INTERNATIONAL CHRISTIAN
GRADUATE UNIVERSITY

DEVELOPING
DYNAMIC
STEWARD-
SHIP

DEVELOPING DYNAMIC STEWARD- SHIP

Raymond B. Knudsen

Abingdon
Nashville

DEVELOPING DYNAMIC STEWARDSHIP

Copyright © 1978 by Abingdon

Library of Congress Cataloging in Publication Data
KNUDSEN, RAYMOND B.
   Developing dynamic stewardship.
   1. Stewardship, Christian--Sermons.   2. Ser-
mons, American. I. Title.
BV772.K58   248'.6   78-7846

ISBN 0-687-10500-5

Scripture quotations noted RSV are from the Revised Standard Version of
the Bible, copyrighted 1946, 1952, © 1971, 1973 by the Division of
Christian Education of the National Council of the Churches of Christ in
the U.S.A. and are used by permission.

The hymn, "Take Thou Our Minds, Dear Lord," that appears on p. 57 was
written by the Reverend William Hiram Foulkes and was published in
The Worshipbook, © 1970 by the Westminster Press.

MANUFACTURED BY THE PARTHENON PRESS AT
NASHVILLE, TENNESSEE, UNITED STATES OF AMERICA

Fifteen sermons dedicated
to the memory and
honor
of
Twelve Noble Men of Faith . . .

E. F. Wright . . . who baptized me as a child of the Covenant in the Congregational Church

H. J. Tedder . . . who exposed me to evangelical Christianity

Ethan Mengers . . . who confirmed my baptismal vows as a Lutheran

Robert Karr . . . who enriched my faith and brought me into the Presbyterian family

Stanley H. Bailes . . . who impressed me with "things really precious"

Otis D. Ironmonger . . . who blessed my marriage

James W. Clarke . . . who taught me human compassion

J. Harry Cotton . . . who provided an example of courage

Jesse Halsey . . . who walked in the steps of the Master

Luther J. Tignor . . . who consummated the marriage of faith and practice

Fred E. Stemme . . . who honored my faith and tradition

R. H. Edwin Espy . . . who brought me into the ecumenical mission

. . . of whom the world was not worthy.

Preface

On the last Sunday in June 1976, as I was about to enter the pulpit of the Cathedral of Saint John in the Wilderness in Denver, Colorado, the Very Reverend Herbert M. Barrall, Dean, asked me what I was going to preach on. I answered, "The Bicentennial." He replied, "I wish you would preach on money instead." I did. The subject was "Cancelled Checks," a sermon which I have preached from pulpits in Maine to Hawaii, from Florida to Alaska.

Clergy everywhere are asking for sermon material on the stewardship of resources. Here, then, are fifteen sermons that I have shared with members of the household of faith in churches in every state of the union and in international congregations of a dozen countries around the world.

I pray that these may be helpful tools in developing an appreciation of resources and support for Christian mission across the nation and around the world.

Contents

Cancelled Checks

"Do not lay up for yourselves treasures on earth, where moth and rust consume and where thieves break in and steal, but lay up for yourselves treasures in heaven, where neither moth nor rust consumes and where thieves do not break in and steal. For where your treasure is, there will your heart be also."
—The Gospel According to Matthew 6:19-21 RSV

Some years ago, three small boys were engaged in a serious conversation on the subject of what they would most like to inherit when their father died. Inasmuch as I was their father, I was very interested in overhearing the conversation.

Raymond, the oldest son, was the first to place his requisition. He wanted my watch. With it, of course, was the chain, the watch fob, and my fraternity key that hung from it.

Silas, the middle son, was interested in my ring. It is a rather sentimental thing inasmuch as over the first fifteen years of our married life, the diamonds graced their mother's finger. She was disappointed at the wedding—not in the groom, thank God, but in the ring—as she preferred a solid gold band. So on the fifteenth wedding anniversary, we exchanged rings; and the diamond cluster in my ring is from the wedding band their mother once wore. Si wanted dad's ring.

Well, when you take away a man's watch and you take away his ring, there isn't much left, is there? But with eyes as large as saucers and as radiant as the sun, Mark, the youngest son, said: "I want all of dad's checks!" The oldest boy responded: "Mark, you wouldn't get a thing! They are worthless! There is nothing of value there!" Certainly he knew the familiar refrain:

> There's nothing left to me
> From last month's salary.
> I live in memory
> Among my cancelled checks.

In defense of Mark's request, there is perhaps something here of greater value than most tend to believe. Actually, in my cancelled checks there is a story of my life—the only autobiography I will ever write. A record of my hopes and dreams. A record of my values and priorities. A record of purchases and expenditures. A story in every transaction, and a signature on every page.

Consider your cancelled checks. What do they say of you? Your life? Your values? Your priorities? Your hopes? Your dreams? Your faith? Let us page through a month of cancelled checks and discover those things most earnestly believed among us.

We Believe in the Home

Here is a big one! Oritani Savings and Loan Association. Three hundred, twenty-nine dollars and thirty-seven cents! This is the payment on the mortgage including principal, taxes, interest, and insurance. For most families it represents a fourth to a third of the family income. And just think, I have only two hundred and thirty-four more payments to make, and the house is all mine.

Whether we buy or lease, we believe in the home. Even in a society that boasts of free love and open marriage, we place great emphasis on the family residence. This is perhaps the most hopeful sign in our culture today. In spite of drastic changes, the home occupies a significant place in our culture. Remember the verse:

> Home is not merely four square walls
> 'though with pictures hung and gilded.
> Home is where affection calls
> Filled with shrines the heart has builded.
> Home! Go watch the faithful dove
> Sailing 'neath the heavens above us.
> Home is where there's one to love,
> Home is where there's one to love us.

We, the American people, believe in the home.

We Believe in Transportation

Let us look again to our cancelled checks. Here is another big one. General Motors Acceptance Corporation. The payment on the automobile. The car salesman insisted that this is probably the second largest investment we will make in our lifetime, and even in inflationary times the prices increase to ensure his credibility.

Firm is our faith in the family limousine. Whether insurance doubles in price, or gasoline increases to a dollar and a quarter a gallon, we are a mobile society; and neither the cost of cars nor operational expenses will change that.

Drive through suburbia, and one is impressed with the fact of our faith in private transportation. There are two garage doors on the front of almost every home, several cars in most driveways, and competition for right-of-way at every intersection.

In designing our homes, we tend to provide more cubic area for our automobiles than for our children. Transportation represents an important part of our daily lives. We believe in private cars.

We Believe in Education

Looking again to our cancelled checks we discover still another significant one. It is the payment for education. Whether the remittance is through real estate taxes or tuition and fees payable to an institution of learning, education has a high priority in our society and provides a great challenge to us as parents to equip our children for opportunities and responsibilities in the future.

The educational processes enlarge with each generation. The floor for a minimum education has elevated from the grade school to the high school, to junior college, to university, to graduate school, and on to continuing education courses, institutes, seminars, and workshops. Some, if not all, of these are utilized by folk in many walks of life, as most are determined to make the future better than the past. We believe in education.

We believe in the home. We believe in private transportation. We believe in education. There they are—an obvious presence in our checkbooks and of great significance among our cancelled checks.

Strange, we do not sing very often of the home or the automobile or even of education except when we attend rallies and reunions and stand for the alma mater. We do, however, sing often of our faith: "My faith looks up to

Thee"— "I surrender all!"— "Christ for the world we sing!
The world to Christ we bring!" But where is the evidence of
our faith in our checkbooks?

Is Our Religion Important?

Throughout my pastoral ministry I was often called upon
by parishioners for documentation concerning their
financial support of the church. They were being audited
by the Department of Internal Revenue and needed
documentation for their gifts to the church. When I
suggested that they refer to their cancelled checks, the
almost universal reply was, "We don't write checks for
anything that small."

In my travels across the nation and around the world, I
have followed with interest the offertory proceedings in
hundreds of local churches. There is no place in the world
where the dollar marches with greater dignity than in the
church. In my area it costs one dollar and fifty-cents to cross
the George Washington Bridge. It costs four dollars per
person to attend Radio City Music Hall, regardless of age.
It costs up to five dollars and fifty cents for tolls to the John
F. Kennedy International Airport—one way! It is interesting how large a one dollar bill appears to people as they sit
behind stained glass windows

On a visit to Phoenix, Arizona, where I have four
grandchildren, the five of us stood at the curbing each
evening to purchase treats from the Good Humor Man.
The last time I left Phoenix, early in the morning, I said to
my daughter-in-law, Marcia, "Here is a dollar that I am
placing on the refrigerator for the Good Humor Man when
he comes tonight." John, then six years old, looked up at
me and said, "You can't buy much for a dollar anymore,

Granddad." Even a six-year-old child knows the limitations of a dollar bill. But how large it appears when it becomes a gift, especially in church.

We say: "I believe!"—"Christ is the answer!"—"Jesus is the hope of the world!" But where is the evidence of that faith, that hope, in our checkbooks?

The Importance of Our Support

In Surabaja, Indonesia, I visited a center where our churches are engaged in mission through a hospital, a clinic supervised by a midwife, a school, and a handcraft shop. The average family of the area consists of ten persons—father, mother, and eight children. The average family income is twelve dollars a month. Adjacent to the church facility, there was a room where small children were copying letters in English, to be sent to benefactors in the United States. I asked my host, "How much does a sponsor give in support of this program?" His answer: "Fifteen dollars each month." I continued, "How much does each child, or family, receive?" His answer: "Six dollars and fifty cents." I thought how wonderful it was that families in need could receive help from persons a half a world away, and secretly I offered a prayer of thanksgiving. But my host continued, "If the money were to come through Church World Service, we would receive fourteen dollars and fifty-five cents of each fifteen-dollar gift!"

Across that vast chain of islands forming the developing nation of Indonesia, I saw, with economy and efficiency, the mission of the church as participating denominations accomplished that which no one can do alone. Certainly the words of Jesus were being fulfilled. "Greater works than these" are being accomplished in this century of progress.

At Upi, high in the mountains above Cotabata in the Philippines, where armed struggle closes almost daily the only passage route, I visited a mission station located some twenty-five miles from the nearest telephone. There was a hospital with a native surgeon. Lines of folk were waiting for treatment, most barefoot, and they had walked days on end for care, an encouraging word, and the healing processes. In this village there was no electricity, but there was a school. There was no threater but there was a church. There were no modern farming implements, but there was a cooperative providing seed, fertilizer, and milling processes to increase the incomes for diligent farmers. The mystery of the Nazarene became known and real, as now they would have bread.

In developing nations, and in areas that need to be developed within our nation, the church provides hope. Yet, its resources are inadequate. Its strength is unequal to the task. It cannot minister as it must. It cannot exercise its mission without our support.

"The fields are already white for harvest" (John 4:35). Never have the opportunities for mission been as great. Never have resources been as inadequate. We, as Christians, tend to be overly impressed by what we give, not because we give much, but because we give often. Jesus' words in the Sermon on the Mount were these: "Where your treasure is, there will your heart be also."

What is your treasure: Your home? Of course. Your automobile? Surely. Education? Certainly. The church? Well, hardly. We simply do not adequately fund the mission of Christ in these times.

Look at your checkbook. Review your cancelled checks. Consider your priorities. Examine your faith.

Give the work of Christ and his church a proper place in your family budget.

How deep is your commitment to Christ?

How deep is your commitment to his Church?

How deep is your commitment to the ecumenical mission?

The answer is in your cancelled checks!

A Model of Faith
to Return Home To

"I will arise and go to my father."
— The Gospel According to Luke 15:18 RSV

The Greatest Story Ever Told is reported to be that of Jesus of Nazareth. The narrative of his birth, baptism, ministry, death, and resurrection is without parallel in human history; and whether we follow the details through the printed word, spoken word, or graphic portrayals on stage or screen, it is a dynamic tale.

But there is another story that comes to my mind when I see or hear those words, because it is an account told by the greatest storyteller of all time, and represents the very person of whom *The Greatest Story Ever Told* is written.

Jesus tells the story—it is that of a father and his two sons. Some refer to it as the parable of the foolish son. Some refer to it as that of the jealous brother. Some say it is a fable about a forgiving father. But most identify it as the Parable of the Prodigal Son. While this narrative involves several persons, numerous truths and dramatic incidents, it is a story of a model of faith to return home to.

The Prodigal Son

There are three patterns of faith in this drama. The first is a reckless spirit that has little appreciation for the past, no concern for the future, and primary interest in the present. This pattern is embodied in the younger of the two boys. His style of life was impulsive. His demand of time and eternity was "Give me my share!"

What was his share?

In his home the youngest son considered his share to be a fair proportion of the family wealth. This son would have been pleased with another story that Jesus told, that of the keeper of the vineyard.

You will remember in that text that it was harvest-time, and the grapes were ripening very fast. Some were overripe, and it was important that all be picked at the earliest possible moment. Early in the morning the vineyardman went to the village and hired as many grapepickers as he thought would be required to do the job. At noontime, it was obvious that there were too few hands to complete the task, so he returned to the village to employ several more. Late in the afternoon, it was apparent that the task could still not be completed without additional help. Near the sunset hour, he returned to the village a third time to employ additional helpers. At eventide, the task was done. He gathered the laborers together to pay them for their work, and each received the same wage. Those who worked for only minutes received the same pay as those who had labored through the entire day. The younger son would view this employer with deep admiration and say, "This is my kind of guy!"

This young man's father was a property owner. Perhaps a homesteader for all we know. Through the years he had labored and struggled, worked and saved, and attained a degree of solvency and stature in the community. Certainly most of what the family had acquired belonged to him. But the younger son was not content to accept this. His brother was older. Certainly, as in the case of most families, the elder child matured before his time. The weight of circumstances, responsibility, and work rested upon him. The family enterprise to progress and prosper depended, in part, upon him. Playtime became worktime, and vacationtime, a pursuit of prosperity and productive enterprise. Certainly much of what the family had, folk could well attribute to him. But the younger son was not willing to accept this.

The prodigal son considered his as an unfortunate timing in birth. He had no control over that. The land had been purchased and cleared. Experimentally crops had been planted, cultivated, and harvested, and through trial and error, experience had proven the best way to produce for a good livelihood. Certainly this family was at the peak of the pyramid in agricultural experience, and it did not matter where they had come from or the difficulty of the path over which they had traveled, this family had arrived. They had much. They had reason to be joyful. Life was, after all, to be enjoyed. The younger son believed that.

At this point in time, the prodigal son made two decisions. First, to get what belonged to him. Second, to head out on his own and discover how the rest of the world lived. He placed his requisition. His father honored his request. With reasonably good fortune, he went his merry way.

His motto of life was "easy come, easy go." If the earth's productivity is determined by the elements and chance, why not the productivity of any enterprise? The toss of the dice, is an example. So he threw the dice, and more often than not, they landed in his disfavor. His losings exceeded his winnings. But life was like that. Even when they had planted seed on the farm, some had fallen on stoney soil, some in thorny soil, and some on parched ground. Only a few seeds were destined to become winners. He would stake his future on the games of chance.

His life became lonely, without companionship. At home there had been the family, friends, and probably a mother. While never mentioned, or recognized—as in most domestic situations, she was the mainstay of the domestic scene and a source of assurance and compassion. He needed love. He thought that was something he could buy. After all, when it is dark and one is under the covers and cannot see, what difference does it make? To have fun without nagging, without responsibility, without obligation—isn't this the greater good? So red lights illuminated his way. Here the price exceeded the reward.

Soon he began to be in want. He couldn't wager without a wage, and no one would play just for fun. So he would work that he might have money to wager and resources to pay for the fun which he considered essential for every person. After all, this was a pattern for life that could best accommodate his philosophy; and when one wins some and loses some, one makes the best of it. Eat, drink, and be merry. A philosophy of life common to man.

The Elder Brother

The second pattern of faith in the parable is that of the cautious spirit. A cautious spirit appreciates the past, is concerned for the future, and is diligent over the responsibilities at hand. This type is embodied in the older of the two boys. His style of life was thoughtful, careful, and deliberate. His position in time and eternity was "Go to the ant, thou sluggard; consider her ways, and be wise" (Proverbs 6:6).

What was one's share? The older son was very much at home in the work-ethic. "He that will not work shall not eat" was a vital concept in his philosphy, and for him impoverishment in this world was a result of laziness. He, too, could turn to the Nazarene and be pleased with a story that Jesus told. It was the story of the rich man whose fields produced a bountiful harvest; and revelling in his success he said, "My soul shall delight itself in fatness." This hero was one who would tear down small barns to build greater barns. For this older son, this was not a story of a rich fool but a biography of a successful and wise man.

When the younger son returned home, the heart of the older boy was filled with bitterness. Though undeserving, the younger boy had received his full share, had had his chance, and had wasted his substance in riotous living.

Through the years this boy of maturity had disciplined himself to laborious hours and long days—fences mended, fields weeded, and stock cared for at farrowing time. Very little time and money were given to parties. Celebrations with friends and neighbors were a luxury which time could not afford. There was much work to do and little time to do it. But the reward for work well done proved it a proper choice in his judgment.

Hard work and very little play was a pattern for life that accommodated his philosophy well and his style of life was that of a cautious spirit.

The Forgiving Father

The third pattern of life in this parable is that of a responsible spirit—a responsible spirit that has deep appreciation for the past, hopeful expectation for the future, and deep regard and appreciation for the opportunities of the present. This pattern, our model, is embodied in the life of the father of the two boys. His style of life was patient. His requisition of time and eternity is verbalized in the prayer attributed to Francis of Assisi:

> Lord, make me an instrument of your peace.
> Where there is hatred, let me sow love;
> Where there is injury, pardon;
> Where there is doubt, faith;
> Where there is despair, hope;
> Where there is darkness, light;
> Where there is sadness, joy.
>
> O Divine Master, grant that I may not so much seek,
> To be consoled, as to console,
> To be understood, as to understand,
> To be loved, as to love
> For it is in giving, that we receive;
> It is in pardoning, that we are pardoned,
> It is in dying, that we are born to eternal life.

Social instinct ran high in this man of mature faith. He, too, could appreciate a story from The Great Teacher—the story of the good Samaritan. In that drama, a traveler, possibly on a route the Samaritan had traveled many times, was accosted by thieves. He was left exhausted, bruised from head to toe, bleeding, and completely destitute as he had resisted them with all his might. While lying in the road, he had gained nothing more than sympathetic glances from a priest and a Levite, both busy and thoroughly convinced that something ought to be done about things like this, but not having the time or the inclination, they chose not to become personally involved. But a stranger, a foreigner, convinced that God had made of one blood all nations of folk to dwell on the face of the earth, confident that his was a fellowship with the whole of the human family, and impressed with the fact that he was indeed his brother's keeper, proceeded to minister to the victim to the best of his abilities. And not content with just that, he took the injured man to the next village and contracted for the victim's cares to be met until he made a complete recovery. This was the father's kind of guy; and through his lifetime, he had engaged in many acts of kindness even when his one son was prone to say, "It is too expensive" and the other, "Each is just a case of bad luck".

The younger son considered his plight. His work was hard, the hours were long, and the wages were scarcely adequate. Certainly his opportunities were less attractive than those provided by his father to the servants. Here was a faith, a model, and a style of life to go home to. Convinced of the rightness of this course, he headed homeward with a sense of shame and apologies for improper judgment, unwise decisions, and poor choices. Impoverished in body and soul, he was determined to make a new start in life in a servant's role.

Upon returning home, while still a distance away, his father saw him, and with a heart filled with joy, poured out his love in gifts, food, and celebration.

Against the vocal objections of the older son and the honest reservations of the younger son, the father could only respond, as a disciple of Christ: "What man is there of you, whom if his son ask bread, will he give him a stone?" (Matthew 7:9)

In this great drama, made articulate in the words of the Savior and duplicated thousands of times over in every age and nation around the world, we discover a model of faith to return home to. As younger children, reckless with resources, materials, and opportunities; as older children, conservative, cautious and covetous; we need to return to the faith of respectable, reasonable, and responsible stewardship. As Christians and parents, we need to respond to human needs in a direct and forthright manner. As stewards and family members, we must support those to whom we delegate responsibility to serve in our behalf in the name of the Blessed Master. As friends and neighbors, we must seek justice, exercise mercy, and walk humbly forward as true disciples of Jesus Christ.

On Being Good Enough

"And when he was gone forth into the way, there came one running, and kneeled to him, and asked him, Good Master, what shall I do that I may inherit eternal life?"
—The Gospel According to Mark 10:17

The teachings of Jesus of Nazareth are evidenced by his sermons, his parables, his prayers and his personal encounters with individuals along the way. His is anything but a cloistered life; and in his journeys from Galilee to Jerusalem, he is continually with people. Some are old, and some are young. Some are healthy, and some are diseased. Some are well adjusted to society, and some are deviates from the norm. Some are people of means, and others are destitute of all worldly goods. Each enrolled in the drama of primitive Christianity; became an instrument to an understanding of Jesus and the meaning of the Christ event in human history.

One important person appears just preceding the triumphal entry into the city of Jerusalem, in an incidental event related by Mark. This encounter is squeezed into the press of a single moment—a moment of preparation, excitement, and change—a moment at the end of three years of basic ministry and the decisive events which were to make Calvary the pivotal point of reference in the salvation process. The person is the rich young ruler who asked life's most significant question: "What shall I do that I may inherit eternal life?" Another of the Gospel writer's penned it in these words: "What good thing shall I do, that I may have eternal life?" It is a question that not only confronted that rich young ruler, but it is a question which confronts every single individual in the pilgrimage to immortality. "What shall I do?"

Consider the incident. It was an event that revolved around the lives of two good men.

Jesus and the Rich Young Ruler

The rich young ruler came to Jesus acknowledging two significant facts about the teacher from Nazareth. First, he considered that Jesus was upright and that his concept of the good was consistent with his own scale of moral values. Jesus and the rich young ruler were not adulterers. They would kill no one. They respected the property rights of others. Their word was as bond. They were both honest. Their lives were complimentary to their parents in every way. These matters were evident and important in the life of the rich man, and they were evident and important in the life of the Person to whom he had come.

The life-style of each was consistent with their moral values, and each would be comfortable in the presence of the other. Certainly each could honor the other. It is obvious from the record of the event that each had great respect for the other.

Here are two good men. Regardless of their place in geography and history, all may subscribe to this fact.

A second trait of the Nazarene comes into focus through this encounter. Jesus was a master, a leader—one capable of giving orders and seeing that they were thoroughly carried out. The inquirer in this event was one such person as well. History notes him as a ruler both young and wealthy.

The leadership role in the life of Jesus was a role which came through a prophetic witness. Call it ideas or idealism. Every age and geographic area has those who gain influence through ideas. These are the teachers. These are the pioneers. These are creative persons who hew out the patterns of history from designs of their own making. Each crisp new idea has the force of a magnet, and the more creative and effective the idea the greater the number of those who are attracted to it. Jesus was such a leader. Even in times of prayer he was seldom, if ever, entirely alone. With such a capability he could say to one "Come," and he would come; to another "Go," and he would go; and in the course of his public ministry, many came and often he sent them, two by two, to bear his message.

The leadership role in the life of the young man was a role that came through money. The late Adam Clayton Powell called it "green power." Affluence makes for influence. One who has money may be resourceful, and continually one with means may have the wherewithal whereby his or her orders may be carried out and purposes may be attained in the manner that person may consider to be the best possible way. This young man's wealth was more than adequate, and there was no need to defraud or shortchange those who carried out his bidding. All of the commandments he had observed from his youth. This attests to his goodness. It is evidence of a fine and noble leader.

So here, on the outskirts of Jerusalem, we have two good men—we have two good leaders. However, one feels inadequate, imperfect in the presence of the other; and the one with "green power" turns to the Master of ideas and ideals and asks; "What shall I do that I may inherit eternal life?" It is a unique question because it is a personal one. He does not ask, What shall one do? Rather, he asks, What shall I do? While the question was specific in terms of the single person, the answer Jesus gave is universal in scope. His answer falls in two parts. First, enter into a sense of community with people. Second, enter into a sense of community with God.

A Sense of Community with People

Affluence tends toward separateness. The master of wealth separated from those who did his bidding. Traditionally we have referred to these groupings as living on alternate sides of railroad tracks. Those of means we have referred to as folk living on the right side of the track. Those without means as living on the wrong. Folk, then, are divided between those who live on the hill and those who live in the ghetto of impoverishment. There is little doubt that Jesus thoroughly believed that this should not be.

Jesus had a strong sense of community and was pained by disparity. Strange, as folk look at the Christian experiment or enterprise and sense the urgency for community, they always consider the results to be degrading instead of upgrading, impoverishing instead of enriching. One need read little of Jesus to discover how wrong we are in sustaining such an assumption. The Christian enterprise was progress—not loss.

For those who were diseased it was to gain health. For those who were naked and cold it was to be clothed. For those who were hungry it was to have food. In the whole

Christian enterprise I cannot find a single loser! Progress and gain, indeed.

Jesus, then, responds to the rich young ruler: "Sell what you have. Give to the poor." Let me put it in still other words. Gain a sense of community with people! Relate to people. Develop a sense of oneness and a sense of belonging to the human family.

Half of our world does not know how the other half lives. And as the world shrinks in size and we emerge into the global village, the problem becomes even more complex. If we think there is cultural shock within our society, think how tremendous it is in a global society. I have seen the differences in a closed society, and I have seen the differences in an open society. I have seen disparity in a society where the per capita annual income averages six and seven thousand dollars a year, and I have seen disparity in a society where the per capita annual income averages six or seven dollars a year. Western civilization sits on a powder keg of potential destruction as a result of the contrast between the haves and the have-nots. And the thing that Jesus was saying to the rich young ruler, he says time and again to folk in every period of history as well as to all with affluence in our society today. Develop a sense of community with people.

Note Jesus' counsel to the rich young man: "Sell what you have." It was as though he were to say: "You are property conscious. Your assets have little or no liquidity." What he is really saying is that property cannot be shared well. Real estate and personal property put you at a dead end in developing capital and resources for people. "Sell what you have." Secure money that you may invest, money that you may have, money that you may give—money that may generate more money for people.

Jesus is saying to a man who is "property poor" get rid of your property. But, note, he doesn't say to give it away. Rather, he says, "sell it." Convert it to cash. Let it have liquidity in order that it may be invested and that it may provide interest as a result of investing. Here the Teacher shares an economic truth.

Having sold these things, Jesus continues, "Give to the poor." Enable them to share in the economic enterprise. If Jesus had intended for them to have property, he would have said to the rich young ruler, "Give your property to the poor." Obviously he knew that transferring a problem from one person to another, or others, was no solution at all.

Sell. Give. Develop the opportunity for investing and sharing. This is the secret to economic growth and development. This is a part of the formula that will bring you, one and all, to eternal life. But the prescription does not end there. He continues, "Come, Follow me."

Note again that Jesus is telling the young ruler to do two things. First, gain a sense of community with people. Second, become involved in community with God.

A Sense of Community with God

Often we assume in life that we can go it alone. It simply is not true. Jesus said, "No one can live to oneself." The interrelationship of Christian souls was illustrated in a most effective way as Jesus pointed to the shrubbery that surrounded his followers pathway. Lifting up the importance of each branch of a plant to the other parts of the same plant he said, "I am the vine, and ye are the branches." You need me. I need you. We need each other. No one can go it alone.

Recently, in a parish in New York State, I was approached by a ruling elder in the United Presbyterian Church in the U.S.A. with the statement: "I wish I could find someone who would tell me that I could be a good Christian without going to church each Sunday." Clergy and laity had discussed the matter with him through the years, and in each event he had confided in them the fact that he liked weekends for himself and his family. For him the only purpose for going to church was to increase the attendance, occupy a pew, and fill the offering plates. Seldom, if ever, had he had an experience of true worship. Church meant little to him beyond counting heads and collecting dollars. Through the years, he had missed the purpose of Christian worship entirely. He did not truly gain a sense of community with others or a sense of community with God through worship. The very reason for coming together had been eclipsed by factors of far less importance than that of fellowship in the faith. The mystery of the body of Christ and the presence of God eluded him in his moments behind stained-glass windows. And that is true of so very many today.

Jesus did not ask the rich young ruler for an offering. That would have been only a small part of himself. Jesus did not ask him to join a vast throng, although minutes later a whole city was to turn out to see him. That would not cause him to be a significant person. Rather, Jesus was asking him to be a part of the rather small, dedicated, and consecrated group of followers that were to give birth to the Christian Church—those whose pilgrimage would take them beyond the Gabbathas and Golgothas of time to life eternal and triumphant. For, indeed, this was the very purpose that the rich young ruler had in coming to the Christ.

Scripture records the fact that he went away sorrowful.

The price was too high. Being good enough to inherit eternal life went beyond the keeping of commandments and the giving of alms. Being good enough to inherit eternal life required the giving of self, engagement in the Christian enterprise, and the setting aside of all material goods that could dim the view of Christian purpose.

So it is with pilgrims in the Way even today. Persons seeking the good life. Folk seeking the full life. People seeking eternal life. Most believe they could be content with a price less than the whole. Good deeds. Kind words. Wholesome attitudes.

But whether they were fisher-folk, landholders, or industrial leaders, the price was the same. Leave nets. Sell land. Dispose of property. Let nothing stand in the way. Deny self. Take up the cross. Follow Christ!

Here, then, is the story of two good men. A story on being good enough to gain eternal life. It may very well be the story of many of us. Many of us who permit property and resources to stand in the way of a full, vital, and vibrant Christian witness. Jesus is saying to each of us: "Sell . . . Give . . . Follow me." This, and this alone, is the secret to being good enough to inherit eternal life.

No Transplants Here

"And he said unto them, Ye will surely say unto me this proverb, Physician, heal thyself: whatsoever we have heard done in Capernaum, do also here in thy country."
—The Gospel According to Luke 4:23

Twenty-five years ago a Mid-western congregation entered into a program to improve their church facilities. Facilities, a half-century old, were in need of updating as a generation had moved from wood and coal to gas and electricity, from a public tramway system to the family automobile. So dramatic was the change over those fifty years that even the well had been covered up in lieu of modern plumbing.

Among the facilities to be updated and improved was the church kitchen. A dozen meals and refreshment servings each week made the kitchen a second home for some of the women in that parish, and therefore these improvements were in high priority with them. For several months they traveled from church to church to see what others had done in order to determine what they might do to have the very best to facilitate their services to Christ and his Church. Upon returning from one such visit they met with the architect and engineers and graphically portrayed their discovery in a certain facility. This was exactly what they wanted. But there were vast differences in location, in size, in the mechanical details of the structure, and much to their disappointment, the architect and engineers had to insist, "There are no transplants here!"

A search committee was seeking diligently for a new senior pastor for its church. On each visit to a prospective candidate they would tour the community, look over the church facilities, and carefully evaluate the program in the parish. After one such visit they returned to their own parish with their new discovery. In a particular city they had found a pastor, a church, and a community which could meet their every need. A call for this particular pastoral leadership would result in the fulfillment of their greatest hopes and dreams. But their denominational ministerial relations committee reminded them, "There are no transplants here!" Facilities, community, and mission simply were not compatible, and effective ministry in one would not ensure a successful ministry in another.

Jesus returned to his own country of Nazareth after considerable time and travel in the pre-Christian world. There was great enthusiasm for his ministry, his miracles, and his vision. With great anticipation relatives and friends said: "What you have done in Capernaum do here also." Much to their disappointment Jesus said, "There are no transplants here!"

Whether it is a church improvement program, a call to a new pastorate, or a visit from the blessed Savior himself, we need to know that there are no transplants here. Renovation, renewal, and redemption require growth and development from the raw materials of a peculiar situation. In some cases, it is a Phoenix emerging out of the ashes of an unfavorable and unmerciful past.

Considering the church, if there are no transplants in terms of facilities, pastoral ministry or gospel, what are the ingredients for meaningful mission today?

Commitment

First, there must be commitment. Often I have said that the Church must belong to Jesus Christ, for no other organization could possibly survive with so shallow a commitment. There is a stronger movement of active to inactive membership than there is from inactive to active membership in the household of faith. Empty pews attest to the indifference of the membership and the fact that the peculiar institution is not sought out by the people who reside in the immediate community. In contrast to the mainline churches, Dean Kelly asks; "Why are the conservative churches growing?" The answer is incorporated in a single word: commitment.

There is a spiritual commitment. In an age of parity and equality, there must be commitment to Jesus Christ as Lord and Savior. Pantheism and humanism permeate our culture and many of our churches. And many ministers in our churches have moved from the position that Jesus is the Lord and Savior to the position that he is one among many and may appear to some as a savior in terms of a unique, peculiar, and particular situation. Our Lord is deemed more important in our culture for festivity than for fact.

There is social commitment. While some may concede that there is, in some situations, a personal salvation, few are convinced that there is a social salvation; few are convinced that society may be redeemed or saved. Jesus' statement "The poor you have with you always" is amplified more readily than his words "Sell what thou hast and give to the poor." Many believe that as long as some can move on to the East Side, have a piece of the pie, economic, social, and political needs are met. But in the church there must be commitment to justice, liberation, and human fulfillment for each person or there is no salvation at all—or even a heaven. Jesus insisted that the kingdom is in you—heaven now.

There is a financial commitment. Some view a personal budget as a thermostat governing religious involvement. I find it a thermometer attesting to the degree of individual commitment to our Lord and Savior Jesus Christ. Those things most vitally believed are supported substantially from the personal budget. Token support in our religious obligations is a product of shallow commitment. The church has inadequate resources for its mission, because we are not committed to the mission in which we are presumed to be willing to share.

In the realm of spiritual commitment there are no transplants. Spiritual, social, and economic concern must rise from our personal experience and involvement.

Concern

A second ingredient of meaningful mission in the church today is concern. Our assumptions of ecclesiastical concern in a world of evangelical need are greatly exaggerated.

A modern poet imagines Jesus visiting Birmingham. There crowds of people racing against time are evident everywhere. Few glance toward the man of Nazareth and none take a deep interest in him at all. The Stranger of Galilee is a stranger to Birmingham. The Christ is in an

environment of indifference. The poet's concluding line is
to the effect that Jesus "cried for Calvary." We shake our
heads, concur that this would surely be true, and conclude
that this applies to Christ's church today as well.

Let us look at the other side of the coin. Let us consider
the society beyond stained-glass windows. Let us consider
the question: Does the church really care?

How many automobiles pass your church each day? How
many pedestrians walk by its front door? How many
children play on its steps? Does each person driving or
riding by, walking along the way, or playing on your steps
discern that you really care about them?

In a parish I served for some twelve years, there was a
woman who was very active in the church's program but
was a member of another church on the other side of the
city. I invited her to transfer her membership and join our
church. The reply was an emphatic no. I inquired, "Why?"
Her answer: "As soon as I join your church, I will become a
forgotten person. Inasmuch as my membership is in
another parish, your people are always polite, concerned
for my well being, and grateful for everything I do. If I join
your church, they will take me for granted. Believe me, I
know. My own church does not care about me!"

In the course of my travels to cities and towns in all fifty of
our states, I have been concerned with the sickness of our
churches—many struggling for their existence, most
scarcely surviving, some actually out of business. Their
facilities have been made into shops, factories, museums,
or what have you. An epitaph over their doors might be:
"We didn't care. We were not concerned."

In inner city areas, suburbs, towns, and villages—among
the parishes that seem to decay—there are churches with

vitality and with strength. They are the exceptions to the rule of depression and decay that I have described. They are centers of activity. Their message is strong. Their mission is sure. Why? Because they care. They are concerned for the community in which they minister, for the people they seek to serve, and they are alert to the issues that cry for solution in their social complex. Churches like that are indestructible, and their communities may never become the product of urban blight, for they provide the life and light that makes for perpetual renewal and hope that never flags.

There are no transplants here. Concern must rise from the caring of souls and from a profound interest in individuals and in the community to which the parish is chartered to serve.

Creative Ministry

A third ingredient for significant ministry in the church today is creative ministry. Across the miles and across the years, we have seen organized religion in depression. Statistics reveal depression in membership, attendance, and financial support. In our cities, in our villages, in open country, and even in our suburbs, there are churches depressed and, in many cases, even closed.

I am pained when I see church buildings no more used for the programs for which they were built and dedicated. Inquiring of folk in these particular areas, I am told that the community has changed—changed in terms of economic, racial, ethnic, national, and social groupings. The churches become desolate in many cases when the population, in fact, has increased by tens, by hundreds, and, in some cases, by thousands of people.

I am sometimes called a "marrying parson" for it is my task to bring together projects and resources, causes and funding, need and finance. There is nothing in the world that cannot be funded. Somewhere there is someone who will fund any particular need. The difficulty is to bring the program need and the funding source into communication with each other. In a sense this describes the church and its mission today.

The resources within the church, organized religion, and institutional structures are great. Needs within our society, our communities, and in areas readily accessible to our congregations are significant and numerous. As members of congregations we have to survey the community, consider the needs, explore the opportunities, and creatively respond with meaningful and effective programs.

View the Christian arena. Jesus of Nazareth began his mission with twelve persons (thank God they did not organize into a committee), but eleven of them, with unflinching devotion, discovered needs, utilized resources, changed the face of the Middle East and made Christianity known to the world. They made it known without newspapers and magazines, radio and television, even without CB radios on their camels and donkeys.

Think what a creative design in ministry could do today in every single parish in this nation—in the world!

Never have opportunities been so great. Never have resources been so vast. Never have needs more seriously plagued the human situation. Never has a creative Christianity had so much to offer!

There are no transplants here. Renovation, renewal, and redemption require growth and development from the raw materials of our peculiar situations. Commitment, concern, and creative ministry are the ingredients for meaningful mission in the church of Jesus Christ today, and world redemption depends upon them. We must not fail!

Three Lessons from
an Ordinary Planter

"Behold, there went out a sower to sow."
                    —The Gospel According to Mark 14:3

The Sermon on the Mount and the Sermon by the Sea
are two great sermons that Jesus preached. We are all
familiar with the Sermon on the Mount as contained in the
Gospel according to Saint Matthew, but we are not always
mindful of the Sermon by the Sea found in Mark. It begins
with these words, "Hearken; Behold, there went out a
sower to sow."

In the parched desert of Palestine, there is little
wonder that these words introduce the Sermon by the
Sea; for if the agricultural process were to succeed in the
primitive age of the Christian period, the sowing,
cultivating, and harvesting would take place somewhere
along the water ways. From a ship, a short way from the
shore of that Galilean sea, Jesus looked beyond the
gathered society to ground broken by a wooden plow and
viewed a farmer sowing seed with measured steps. As the
Master saw the seed falling from the farmer's hands, he
was impressed with the optimisim of the moment and the
disappointment of the process. Most of the seed was
going to waste, even when one was planted in hope. Yet

he considered the validity of the agricultural process, and through it we learn a first lesson from an ordinary planter.

The Importance of Sowing

"Behold, there went out a sower to sow." Seeds leaving the hand of the sower seemed to fall in four directions.

First, some of the seed was carried by the wind and fell in places not even plowed. Easily seen by birds, they came to eat it about as rapidly as it fell to the ground. Ecologists might well say: "Foolish man. You should not plant seed when the wind is blowing. Think of those who could profit from that seed, either by consuming it or planting it." But the Nazarene knew, as all farmers know even now, that if you wait for windless days seedtime will never come.

Second, he noted that some of the seed fell on stony ground, and one cannot visit the Near East without being mindful of the fact that stones dominate the landscape, even in the best kept fields. There is simply no way that either large rocks or clods of dirt can be removed completely or eliminated even through modern mechanized farming. There, on stony ground, the seed would lay, perhaps even germinate as a result of light rain, but the sun would cause it to wilt and die. Here, too, there are those concerned with the plight of the poor and the hungry, who say: "You must be more careful where you plant the seed. Think of those who could profit from the seed either by consuming it or planting it."

Third, he noted that some of the seed fell among thorns—thorns among the clods of dirt, thorns so prickly that the oxen, the asses, and even the farmer would tend to move around them instead of through them. Yet here was the seed, and even when it took root and began to grow, it could not survive as the competition was too keen, the thorny plants too hearty, and the fertility of the soil too sparse to enable the desired plant to endure. And here conservationist might say: "You must be more careful when you plant the seed. Think of those who could profit from that seed either by consuming it or planting it."

Then Jesus discerned that other of the seed fell on good ground, and in his mind's eye he could see it take root, grow, and flourish. At harvest-time some will have increased thirtyfold, some sixtyfold, and some a hundred-fold. And this same farmer, accused of recklessness, carelessness, and foolishness, could respond to the ecologist—to one concerned with the plight of the poor—and to the conservationist with shouts of joy, "This is the product of my labor that confirms the process as worthwhile. In spite of wind, rocks, and thistles, this is a valid process, and it assures me that my work is worthwhile." It was worth his while even when three-fourths of his sowing was doomed to failure.

The first lesson we learn from an ordinary planter is that the agricultural process works, and it is a process which is very much worthwhile. And even today, whether modern farmers sow by hand or use the most sophisticated machinery of the technological age, the process remains unchanged in time. In spite of losses, in spite of risks, the process is worthwhile. Year after year we must continue to plant. Unless we sow, we cannot reap.

This first lesson from an ordinary planter is obvious: If there is to be a harvest, there must be diligent labor exercised in seedtime regardless of the discouraging facts that seem to say, "Save your strength. Three-fourths of what you do will not prove productive."

The Importance of Communicating

Then the Young Man from Nazareth moves to the second lesson from an ordinary planter. Here he addresses his thoughts to those in the field of communication: the newscaster, the teacher, the minister. As percentages seem great against the farmer, they are inclined to be equally great against those who feed the mind and the soul.

First, a word is spoken, competing influences keep it from being heard. There is a knock at the door, the telephone rings, a child cries for attention or affection, or one of the thousand and one distractions emerging in the day steal from our lives a mind attentive to the word. A time analyst will say: "Be careful to use each opportunity to speak in a wise way. Be articulate. Think of those who may profit from the word merely by hearing it or making use of the message."

Second, a word is spoken, and fixed minds and impenetrable prejudices refuse to give it birth. For a brief moment there seems to be a spark of recognition, a discernment of worth, and a responsive chord, but the mind-set of the past prevails over the unfamiliar element of the present and the word bounces from one wall to another down the corridors of time without contributing to the process of knowledge and understanding. A sociologist will say: "You must be careful when you speak to address your speech to those who are open to your teaching. Think of those who could profit from the word merely by hearing it or making use of its message."

Third, a word is spoken and the thought processes weigh it in the scale of consciousness, and it is choked out by an evaluation process that declares from a limited experience that it does not merit the priority of acceptance or credibilty that retains it as a verity of life. The cares of this world, and the deceitfulness of riches, and the lusts of other things entering in, choke the word, and it becometh unfruitful. An ethicist will say: "You must be careful when you speak to address your speech to those whose style of life will accommodate your teaching. Think of those who could profit from the word merely by hearing it and making use of its message."

Then Jesus discerned the word spoken to capable minds and receptive hearts and noted that in some cases it produced thirtyfold, in some cases sixtyfold, and in still other cases a hundredfold. And this same teacher accused of carelessness by the time analyst, of nonselectivity of audience by the sociologist, and of wasting time and breath by the ethicist, shouts of joy, "This is the product of my labor which confirms the process as worthwhile!" In spite of elements of destruction, fixed minds and impenetrable prejudices, appraisals of less than deserving merit, this is a valid process; and it assures me that my work is worthwhile, even though much of my speaking falls on deaf ears.

The second lesson we learn from an ordinary planter is that the teaching process works, and it is a process which is imperative to progress. And even today, whether teachers use the person-to-person method or communicate through the mass communication media, the process remains unchanged in time. In spite of losses, in spite of risks, the process is worthwhile. Certainly we must communicate through the spoken word.

The Importance of Giving

Through the mind of Christ, we move to the third lesson from an ordinary planter. A lesson which relates to the philanthropic process. Here we address our thoughts to those who are engaged in services to others; the poor, the disfranchised, the exceptional persons on the horizon of human need. In response to appeals through the mails, mass communication media, and by personal solicitation, we engage in philanthropic giving. At times it is a local or community agency, at times a church or church-related program, and at times a national or international enterprise.

First, a gift is given, and somewhere along the way, it may be intercepted. Through graft or theft, or less-than-wise investing policies, the value is lost to the humanitarian objective, and a nonbenevolent person will say: "You must be careful how you give your money. Think of those who could benefit from its use by keeping it in the bank."

Second, a gift is given to a seemingly deserving cause. There is great need. The plans seem reasonable and logical, but few respond with generous support. Resources are not sufficient to either provide services or effect change, and it is like the baseball player bunting a ball for a sacrifice play when the bases are empty. An executive of the United Way will say: "You must be careful of the causes you support. Think of those who could have benefited from your gift through an approved agency."

Third, a gift is given where good work could be done, but the agency is poorly staffed, and inadequately organized, and the value goes to lesser goods which are not designed to meet the basic human need calling for strength in redemption and rehabilitation. And an efficiency expert will say: "You must be careful in your giving. Think of those who could have benefited more if you had chosen another cause to support."

Then there is the gift uniquely timed and effectively programmed to produce significant and measurable results with some portions of the gift producing thirtyfold, some sixtyfold, and some a hundredfold. This same philanthropist accused of carelessness by the nonbenevolent, of choosing a lesser good by a United Way executive, and of poor judgment by an efficiency expert, shouts with joy: "This is the product of my sharing. It confirms the fact that my giving is worthwhile."

The third lesson from an ordinary planter is an obvious truth: If the hungry are to be fed, the naked to be clothed, and the poor to be elevated to the plains of hope; we must continue to be generous even though discouraging experiences seem to prove that three-fourths of our philanthropic giving may not be productive at all.

Melodiously, over the airwaves from eternity, echo words of the blessed Master, "Inasmuch as ye have done it unto one of the least of these, my brethren, ye have done it unto me."

Thanks be to God for those who plant, for those who teach, and for those who share generously and unselfishly in the philanthropic and humanitarian processes which may well meet basic material, social, and spiritual needs.

The Prayer Perfect—
or Incomplete

"After this manner therefore pray ye: Our Father which art in heaven, Hallowed be thy name."
—The Gospel According to Matthew 6:9

Today, as every day, the Lord's Prayer is being repeated by millions of people in perhaps every language and dialect known to humankind. Except for few variations, it is universally accepted not only as the prayer pattern for the ages but as the *perfect prayer* as well.

This prayer is recited in worship services and Sunday school classes; it is recited at conventions and conferences; it is recited in churches and homes, and it is included in table graces and bedtime prayers.

In ecumenical gatherings we tend to discern the religious identity of a group in one or two places in the prayer. Not certain of the climate, we wonder to ourselves, "Shall we say debts or trespasses" in the first instance; and in the second, shall we include "For thine is the kingdom, and the power, and the glory, for ever. Amen? And at times there has been a third question, namely, Shall it be "forever" or "forever and ever?" In spite of these questions, there is a sense of community and oneness in such gatherings as we have again and again experienced a sense of participation and belonging in a bond of faith indicative of one Lord, one faith, and one baptism through the saying of the Lord's Prayer.

The Petitions

There are six petitions in the Lord's Prayer and each is simply stated:

1. Thy kingdom come.
2. Thy will be done on earth, as it is in heaven.
3. Give us this day our daily bread.
4. Forgive us our debts, as we forgive our debtors.
5. Lead us not into temptation.
6. Deliver us from evil.

Six specific petitions. Six simple statements. Six requisitions to God. Hopefully, six gifts simply to be received: a better world, providential care, food and clothing, forgiveness and understanding as we forgive and understand, guidance and direction, deliverance and hope.

But did you notice there is a difference in one? The fourth petition is conditional. The measure of the prayer request granted is to be determined by the index of personal experience. The extent of the gift is conditioned by the performance of the individual. It is startling for its difference to all others. Listen to it:

"Forgive us our debts, as we forgive our debtors."

"Forgive us our trespasses, as we forgive those who trespass against us."

"Forgive us our sins, as we forgive those who sin against us."

The fourth petition stands so different from the other five that it causes me to wonder: Has something been added? Is there an interpolation here? Has an editor somewhere in the corridors of history simply appended his own words in "forgive . . . as we forgive our debtors? Forgive . . . as we forgive those who trespass against us? Forgive . . . as we forgive those who sin against us?"

Was one in an editorial process gloating so over his own ability to forgive others that it seemed desirable to amplify his personal experience in "forgive us as we have demonstrated an ability to forgive others"?

Or, is it possible that in the editorial process, one has suffered from wrongdoing and tried desperately for reconciliation only to discern that the person or persons wronged cannot exercise the grace to forgive, and in exercising authority over an interpretation of the perfect prayer, offers an addition in "forgive as we forgive?" It may well be that in the fourth petition something indeed has been added. However, in editorial processes, it is more likely that some things have been omitted, eliminated. And it seems obvious that the rhythm of the prayer perfect has been disrupted by the omission of a phrase from each of the other five petitions. Such omissions might have been:

Thy kingdom come, as we give it entrance.

Thy will be done, as we exercise it.

Give us this day our daily bread, as we share our substance with others.

Lead us not into temptation, as we will not be tempting of others.

Deliver us from evil, as we bring deliverance to others through our life and work.

It seems possible, doesn't it? The fourth petition is so strikingly different from all others that it is logical to assume that either something has been added to the one or some things have been deleted from the other five.

In my childhood days, the lines of a verse were

impressed indelibly upon my mind. While I do not recall them all, two are crystally clear in my memory: "God has no hands but our hands"; and "God has no feet but our feet."

These recollections from my youth cause me to cast my ballot with the theory that editors may have omitted portions of the prayer perfect—for actually the prayer is not perfect at all, unless it is perfected in us. The Lord's Prayer depends upon us. It makes demands on our being perfect.

Consider these petitions again:

The Mandates

Thy kingdom come. Can we assume that the kingdom will come simply out of the blue with no individual initiative whatever? The disciples hoped so, but Jesus insisted that the kingdom of God was in them. He said, "The kingdom of God is in you!" You must make it accessible. Rightfully our prayer must be, Thy kingdom come, as we give it entrance.

Thy will be done. Can we assume that all things are the will of God? Election and predestination are splendid doctrines in the Calvinistic tradition, but does it give us the right to leave all things to God? The woman raped? The child harmed? A race defamed? Can we merely write these things off as the will of God? Jesus' intercession for the woman taken in adultery seems to say it isn't so. Rightfully our prayer must be, Thy will be done, as we exercise it.

Give us this day our daily bread. A prayer for food from on high. Although the manna in the Exodus Story was God-given, the children of Israel were permitted to gather only enough for a single day—food one day at a time during a crisis of want in wilderness wanderings. At the feeding of the five thousand, it was deemed important to share what one had. Jesus insisted before a vast crowd: "You must provide! You must be willing to give!" Beginning with five loaves and two fish, provisions were adequate for a great multitude, twelve basketsful beyond the need of that moment. Now, as then, the prayer must be, Give us this day our daily bread, as we share our substance with others.

Lead us not into temptation. Take us away from the pinnacle of the Temple; the rocky slope of a barren wilderness; and the mountaintop where we may view symbols of progress on the land, in the sea, and in the air. When tempted, Jesus said, "Get thee behind me Satan! Thou shalt not tempt the Lord, Thy God!" Rightfully our prayer must be: Lead us not into temptation, as we are determined not to mislead, misdirect, or misinform—in fact, tempt others.

Deliver us from evil. It would seem to be a petition that would take us out of the world, but in the great intercessory prayer of the master in the seventeenth chapter of John's Gospel, our Lord is praying, not that we be taken out of the world, but that we be delivered from the evil that is in the world—that we indeed be made perfect. Rightfully our prayer must be, Deliver us from evil, as we bring deliverance from evil to others through our life and through our work.

While this may well be our prayer, we all know that we live in a society far too complex for us to complete the mandates inherent in the Lord's Prayer, in and through ourselves. Society is too complicated, issues too hard, circumstances too involved for neat answers or oversimplified assumptions. Actually, it requires the coordinated efforts of a closely knit group—a society of the concerned, a concentrated effort by people woven into a fabric of full commitment.

Returning to the prayer pattern for the ages, we come to the application of the petitions to our lives in society today.

The Implications

Thy kingdom come. A kingdom covers a broad span, is inclusive of many people, and transcends the ethnic, racial, and cultural; the economic, social, and political strata in each society. Yet we know in this twentieth century of progress that a kingdom concept more limited than the global village is not practical for the seventies, eighties, and nineties. We have entered into a universal community which Wendell Willkie described as *One World.* The hope for the kingdom lies, therefore, in the individual working through the church to effectively bring the kingdom of God to fruition.

Thy will be done. Here, too, the fulfillment of the will of God in these times requires something more than the divine purpose evidenced in single or remote instances. A ground swell of response to the will of God is imperative if there is to be change—renewal in society, growth in economy, and effective democratic processes in these times. Here, again, it takes the coordinated efforts of many to provide impact for the fulfillment of the will of God in the arenas of human cultures today.

Give us this day our daily bread. We pray for rain. The sweat on the brows and the callouses on the hands of those who till the soil is certainly not without significance. Yet, when the nations' larders are full, and resources more than adequate, there is no reason to assume that everyone will have food. Hunger exists in a world of plenty and of waste. This is a sad commentary on our times. Our problem is basically a problem of geography, of economics, politics, and distribution. While it may not always have been true, it is true today that there is adequate food to feed the world's people. However, there is not the dedication or determination among those who *have* to provide for those who *have not*. The petition in this instance demands that we place in gear the power and the machinery that will bring the world's substance, to fair distribution, and no one can do this alone. There is the need for ecumenical organization—a consoliated effort unlimited to national, political, racial or economic borders.

Forgive us our debts. It is a fact that those who are the most indebted in our society sense the least indebtedness. Many feel little indebtedness to society, the system that makes success possible, the people who enable one to stand and prosper. Some who contribute the most to an individual's progress receive little or no reward. Through this inconsistency, there is a wrong factor. There needs to be a turnabout, a turnabout that will bring recognition of and appreciation for everyone whether we think in terms of economics, morals, or ethics. The church stands in an unusual and strategic position to provide a full understanding of the Gospel and to sustain a meaningful mission to the healing of these times.

Lead us not into temptation. The petition assumes that there is another way, an alternative to injustice, bondage, and inequality. There is a temptation to reserve the better part for ourselves. This at the expense of all others. Frequently at the pain and destruction of someone else. Such a course is inexcusable in the Christian scheme. We simply must not submit to the lesser good. Our theological perspective must enable us to establish a more favorable climate for overcoming rivalry, jealousy, and hatred.

Deliver us from evil. So complex is the human situation

that deliverance for one is impossible; for few, a rarity; and for all, imperative if we are indeed to attain the full and complete will of God. No person stands alone. Evil must be eradicated in order that each may attain the Divine purpose. This is the task of organized religion and the mission of the church.

The prayer of the Lord becomes perfected in us. Surely the pattern is in the mind of Christ, but the implementation is dependent upon those who assume the role of Christian disciples. And the task is too large for anyone, yet the participation of each is of supreme importance.

How may we attain our goal? When will the Kingdom come? How can God's will be done? The answer, at least a partial answer, comes in Christ's Holy Church and our participation in its life and work. It comes through our personal support enabling it to carry out the implications of the gospel here and now.

> Take thou our minds, dear Lord, we humbly pray;
> Give us the mind of Christ each passing day;
> Teach us to know the truth that sets us free;
> Grant us in all our thoughts to honor thee.

A Contrast Between Two Extremes
And Shades in Between

"Thou shalt love the Lord thy God with all thy heart, and
with all they soul, and with all thy strength, and with all thy
mind; and thy neighbor as thyself."
—The Gospel According to Luke 10:27

Suppose someone were to ask you the question Who is
my neighbor? What would you say?

This question was put to Jesus, and his answer has
become one of the most interesting stories in all history. It
is a parable that begins with these words: "A certain man
went down from Jerusalem to Jericho," and almost
everyone knows the rest of the story. Usually it is known as
"the Parable of the Good Samaritan. I like to call it A
Contrast Between Two Extremes and Shades in Between.

The Characters in the Story

We begin with a certain man who went from Jerusalem
to Jericho. We know little about him. Nothing about his
size or shape, his color or race, his faith or his politics. Most
would assume that he was a Jew, but Jesus does not say. We
only know that he was a man of likely means, and a man of
spirit. If he were not a man of means, he would never have
been robbed. If he were not a man of spirit, he would not

have endeavored to preserve and protect his possessions. He wanted what he had. What he had he wanted to keep. What he had he wanted to keep from others. His philosophy was clear and is readily understood. "What is mine is mine, inasmuch as I have worked for it. What is mine is mine, and I am going to keep it. What is mine is mine, and you cannot have it." While it seems a reasonable, logical philosophy, it is a philosophy that left him injured, impoverished, and broken in spirit. Ordinarily, he was a man of respect, of dignity, and of means. At the side of this road, he was an outcast—avoided and rejected.

The second person in our roll call was a certain Samaritan. He was a man. He was a foreigner. He was a person of some means. Why he was not one who fell among thieves no one can say. It may be because of the time of the day. It may be because of his race or nation. It may have been because of his size or life-style. It may be simply because he was one who would not travel in isolation from all others, would make certain to position himself only a short distance behind or in advance of others. Obviously, this Samaritan was a kindly soul; for as he approached the man who fell among theives, he was moved to compassion, stooped to the victim's weakness, nursed his wounds, and took him to a place of renewal and hope. Here in contrast to the victim, this Samaritan was prone to say, "What is mine is yours if you need it." Perhaps this was one reason why he was not attacked or molested in his travels on this highway of life.

Now, between these two men, there are many shades of difference. Consider the robbers. Some would say that they did not believe in working for a living. But they did. In fact, their's was hard work. It required the ability to appraise. It required the ability to fight. It required the ability to overcome. Without reservation their point of view philosophically was, "What is yours is mine, if I can get it."

Consider the priest. He was a good man. He was schooled in religion. He knew the Scriptures. He was respected as a leader. He certainly preached of good works, and it is very possible that the good works of the man of Samaria were the product of this type ministry. The priest looked to the victim. He was concerned over human problems. He hoped for a better world. But he did not stop. He did not nurse the wounds of one afflicted. He did not engage in a ministry of personal rehabilitation. We do not know his reasons. We can only speculate. It may have been because the victim was not of his faith or because a ministry of this type compassion was below the dignity of his office as a priest. Seemingly the priest is saying "What is mine is mine to be used for a religious service."

Consider the Levite. The Levite's role in the narrative of the Master is about the same as that of the priest. He paused, looked at the plight of the unfortunate individual, shook his head, and probably said, "Someone ought, to do something about this." Perhaps they need more officers to patrol the highway. Perhaps they need a more developed highway with fewer turns, more open spaces, and broader thoroughfares, in order that no one be taken by surprise. Perhaps he is less guilty of a sin of omission than the priest who preceded him. If a priest doesn't care, why should he? The Levite, with the priest, is saying, "What is mine is mine, and I am responsible to use it for the cause for which it was provided."

Consider the innkeeper. He, too, was a fine and noble man. His business was to be a good host, a gracious man, and a respectable spirit. He is depicted as being a man of integrity and a man of trust. He knew how to care for people, and he knew how to care for families. He knew how to take care of his business, too. For when a man from Samaria told him to do something, he did it. And he could be trusted to give a good accounting of it as well. His occupation and mode of life were saying: "What is mine is yours, if and when you need it, as long as you can pay for it."

The Pharisee and Jesus

The biographical details in this narrative are not complete if we confine the story to the tale that Jesus told. The story does not attain its full significance until we consider the one who asked the initiating question and the person to whom the question was directed.

It was a Pharisee who asked the question "Who is my neighbor?" He was typical of many of us who ask questions and seek answers; questions posed to amplify position and answers to project personal integrity. Few questions are in search of truth, and few questioners are seekers of truth.

"Which is the great commandment of the law?" The answer was obvious: "Thou shalt love the Lord thy God with all thy heart, and with all thy soul, and with all thy mind, and with all thy strength" (Matthew 22:37). The Pharisees believed they were doing that. Their professional life attested to this sacred condition. But Jesus, in responding to the question, continued: "And the second is like unto it, Thou shalt love thy neighbor as thyself" (verse 39). Even this struck a responsive chord, for the Pharisees were neighborly to each other and neighborly in their Jewish communities. In order to reinforce the importance and value of neighborliness within their fraternity they asked, "And who is my neighbour?" The surprise in the response came when community extended beyond the cloistered area of their common life, even to Samaria.

The Storyteller

Consider now our Lord. While we have assumed that the focus in the story is on the man from Samaria, it is actually a story focused on the Man from Nazareth and his philosophy. Through it he reveals three significant truths at the heart of Christian stewardship.

First, we are responsible for the whole of life. Christianity does not afford the luxury of considering only the causes which relate to our type, sex, clan, community, tribe, or nation. We live in a world of people and in a world in which each one of us is responsible to and for others. In this we need to remember that the story of the Good Samaritan, in part, is a result of timing. Because the Samaritan approached the scene when he did, the story took on the character of restoration and renewal. Had he appeared on the scene a bit earlier, the story may have been one of intervention and arbitration. If he had appeared a bit later the event may never have occurred.

The Good Samaritan was a man who was concerned with people and he was dedicated to the task of bringing out the very best in them. Through him Jesus endeavors to teach us that as Christians we are responsible to and for people at all times, in all places, regardless of the circumstances.

Second, we are responsible for particular life. Most relationships in life are one to one. Each is unique in the fact that at certain moments in history there is only one person who must act and at times we are that person. The man from Samaria was not given a choice either in terms of the time, the place or the circumstances. A crisis had occurred. A person was in desperate need. It appeared that he was the only person available to help. Circumstances demanded his personal response, and he responded. He surveyed the situation, analyzed the need, went into action, and moved in a direction which would spell progress for both him and the victim.

We might assume that the story would end there. Surely the man from Samaria had done well. No one could possibly deny the fact that he was a good man. But, thank God, the story does not end here.

In this historic drama, Jesus understands that personal responsibility cannot be confined or confining. No one knew how long healing would take or how involved the rehabilitation process might become. Had the man from Samaria assumed the total responsibility he may have been confined and limited in his efforts for days, weeks, or even months. Certainly he had a responsibility to the victim, but he also had a responsibility to others and to himself. Jesus does not overlook these facts in his story.

This parable takes a new twist at the desk of the innkeeper. Delegated responsibility. The man from Samaria concedes that there are hands more capable, more patient, and more readily available than his to complete the rehabilitation process. With a firm commitment of pledged support, he delegates that responsibility to someone else through the financial security he is willing to provide. Funds given—funds pledged.

In this parable of the Good Samaritan, Jesus insists that stewardship requires both our personal involvement as Christians as well as our assurance of the availability of the services of others in effecting redemptive processes in a total society.

Individuals Today

Individually there are things we can do and things we must do. And there are things which we cannot do and should not do. Yet there are things which must be done. These are the things which will only be done as we make possible the doing of them.

Increasingly, the assisting and rehabilitating processes in a complex society have, of necessity, become delegated. The development of organizations, institutions, and agencies have made possible, in theory at least if not always in practice, the availability of the very best services and care that can possibly be brought to the victims of circumstances and those in desperation who are in need of tender loving care.

In our society of specialization we realize, too, that our greatest gifts may not be commensurate with life's important needs at any particular moment in history. To assume a samaritan role for the whole of the healing, rehabilitating process may not be the best solution to every problem. Our service, in fact, may prove to be a disservice to someone else as well as to ourselves. But through delegated responsibility, and our generous funding ministries of redemption, reconciliation, and rehabilitation, we come a step farther toward the kingdom of God and the mission to which we as Christians are called.

Who is my neighbor? Neighbors are those who have and those who have not, those who are strong and those who are weak, those upon whom we may depend and those who may depend upon us. Through personal involvement, and through an exercise of good stewardship through our financial support of humanitarian, philanthropic and Christian services, we assume the role of good samaritans in our twentieth-century society.

Three Words with Promise

"Ask, and it shall be given you; seek, and ye shall find;
knock, and it shall be opened unto you: For every one that
asketh receiveth; and he that seeketh findeth; and to him that
knocketh it shall be opened."
—The Gospel According to Matthew 7:7-8

The names of Philip Arnold and Jack Slack probably are
engraved in history as the greatest con artists in all time.
Carefully they gleaned about fifty thousand dollars in
imperfect diamonds, sapphires, and rubies from European
markets; seeded a mine field surrounding Black Butte,
Wyoming; and interested William C. Ralston of the Bank of
California; August Belmont, Henry Seligman, General
George B. McClellan, and General Benjamin F. Butler in
investing millions of dollars through the California and
New York Mining and Commercial Company in an enterprise that seemed promising for such assayers as Tiffany
and Henry Janin who estimated the company's proceeds to
be a million dollars a month. Give and you shall receive,
invest, was the corporate message, but the yield never
resulted in dollars and cents; only in disappointment after
disappointment. Stones that glittered were not diamonds,
gold, sapphires, or rubies. The only gems in the minefield
were those planted by the perpetuators of the hoax.

Some assume that this is the type of hoax perpetrated by the Teacher from Nazareth who said: "Ask, and it shall be given you; seek, and ye shall find; knock, and it shall be opened unto you: For every one that asketh receiveth; and he that seeketh findeth; and to him that knocketh it shall be opened." They tend to say, "I don't believe it!" or "It cannot be true!" or "Prove it!"

Granted, these simple promises from Jesus found in Matthew 7 seem inconsistent with the realities of life as most of us believe we experience them, and they provide another reason why many assume that the church and its message are impractical in these times.

Are they? Are they truly inconsistent with the realities of life? Do they indeed provide another reason for some to believe that the church and its message is unimportant and irrelevant to these times? Let us put them to the test of actual practical experience: "Ask, and it shall be given you."

Ask

Early in my pastoral ministry I served in a small community in western Illinois. It was a rural area on the banks of the Mississippi River and most of the inhabitants derived their livelihood from the productivity of the soil. In addition, there were some services to people—services normal to the activity and productivity of the agricultural enterprise; government, education, and commerce; and the standard components typical of community life and activity the world over. There was one difference, however. The community was deficient in health services, and there was no hospital in Hancock County, Illinois.

We convened a number of community leaders in

Carthage, the county seat, who shared our concern for improving health services, and the meeting resulted in organizing a committee to launch a campaign to build a hospital. In the course of two years, Carthage Memorial Hospital became a reality. Six hundred thousand dollars was required in local funding, and when these funds were fully committed, they qualified to be matched by like amounts by the state of Illinois and the United States Government. In the course of our efforts, the various facets of development were at work to enable the committee to reach the funding goal. There were opportunities for memorials, special gifts, pledges over a period of three years, and benefits of numerous types by community action groups.

One Sunday afternoon we spent perhaps two hours in a farmhouse in the Hunt-Lima District, an area protected by levies, drainage ditches, and pumping stations along the Mississippi River explaining the importance and the advantage of hospital resources to folk in that rural county particularly in case of serious illness or a disaster. The need was well-documented, the cause persuasive, and the opportunity without precedent there. Near the conclusion of our conversation my host said, "Let me see that list of special gifts again." He looked over the list carefully, and glancing in his wife's direction said, "What do you say we provide the money for one of the operating rooms?" This was, of course, before the women's liberation movement; and like the average wife she responded, "Anything you want to do is perfectly all right with me!"

The cost of a hospital operating room was $27,500. Certainly a contribution beyond my fondest expectation. In fact, it was beyond my estimate of their financial means, and when the decision was firm I inquired, "How do you plan to pay for this?" His reply: "I'll give you a check for it right now." Indeed he did. Upon receiving the check, I folded it, and as I placed it in my vest pocket, I said, "Friend, why have you never done anything like this for your church?" The answer was simple. "No one ever asked me!"

Is this not true for most parishioners up and down church street today? Unless there has been a fire or flood, an earthquake or tornado, a new building or extensive renovation program, most persons go through their entire church-related lives without a meaningful challenge, without an invitation to respond with significant support for Christian mission and witness.

"No one ever asked me!"

"Ask, and it shall be given you."

We need to define our askings, and these askings must not be confined merely to bricks and mortar, sanctuaries or facilities, capital funds or endowments.

Today we ask for:

- $500 to provide oil and gasoline for a volunteer to deliver "meals on wheels."
- $5,000 to sustain a Christian witness on a state university campus.
- $10,000 to strengthen a multiracial, multiethnic, and multilingual ministry in the inner city area of one of our largest metropolitan areas.
- $25,000 to support a "seed for work" program in Southeast Asia, where advanced and improved farming methods may ensure productivity and provide a solution to the problem of hunger.
- $50,000 to establish a training institute in Africa that will improve skills among black workers enabling them to

occupy the roles that they will be required to fill when apartheid becomes a matter of history.

- $75,000 to provide clinical services in the South Pacific that will bring medical care to a struggling Christian community seeking recognition in an unfriendly environment and a solution to the physical hardships which result from disease and pestilence.

"Ask, and it shall be given you!"

Seek

"Seek, and ye shall find."

In a midwestern city we became acquainted with a young girl who was enrolled in a primary class in our Sunday school. She was approaching her teens, was unusually attractive, and had a winsome smile; but she was retarded. Her mother had taught Sunday school at the primary level for a number of years, and both the mother and daughter had stayed at the primary age level in order that that charming girl could attend Sunday school. In pastoral concern, I encouraged them to progress from age level to age level with the years in order that the growing young girl would be able to relate to folk of her own age and in order that folk of her age may have the opportunity and the privilege of relating to a person with her unusual qualities and limitations. The decision was affirmative, and it proved to be a most rewarding experience.

In the State of Illinois, in those days, classes were conducted in the public schools for educable retarded persons when an enrollment potential for a particular age group exceeded twelve persons. In most down-state communities, the number was not this great. And classes were not available for trainable children regardless of age or number. The teacher in our Sunday school was an officer in the local chapter of the Association for Help to Retarded Children and shared her deep concern with me. They needed a meeting place, they needed qualified teachers, and they needed funding. In our parish we had space, and we had a concern which laid the foundation for our search.

We began our recruit for teachers among retirees, folk whose skills were not outdated and folk whose modest incomes required subsidy for a reasonable life-style consistent with their vocational experience. In the course of several weeks, we were in touch with two persons who were amiably qualified and whose interest matched their capability.

With space, concern, qualified leadership, and modest funding needs, we sought out the sources that were in a position to provide grants to make our dreams come true. Indeed, they did, and for more than five years three such classes were conducted daily in our church. When our plant proved inadequate—the program grew too large for our facilities—the classes moved to a school of their very own.

Similar opportunities, as broad as human need, prevail in our society, and often because we simply do not seek the solution to the problems that make life less than good or acceptable for a great number of people.

"Seek, and ye shall find!" Seek solutions to the problems of the elderly who struggle for independence and against conditions which would cause them to become institutionalized.

Seek resolution to the problems of our youth who become delinquent in a society that deprives them of respect for their integrity, appreciation of their abilities, and open doors to opportunity.

Seek answers to the problems of inequality in our society which make second-class citizens out of first-class people because of their race, sex or cultural traditions.

"Seek, and ye shall find!"

Knock

"Knock, and it shall be opened unto you."

In my pastoral ministry in New York, the parish area included the first community college opened in that state. It was still in its infancy as an institution, and I was anxious that the curriculum include the science of religion and a basic understanding of the Christian faith as well as the exact sciences, philosophy, and the arts. I wrote to the president of the Orange County Community College and requested permission to develop a program in the church facilities, comparable to a student foundation program, in which courses in religion could be offered each quarter with college credit. Several days later the president of the college called my office for an appointment, and when we met, his first words were these: "You have a grand idea. But why don't we offer these courses on the campus?" This was far better than I had hoped for, and the very next quarter, a course was offered in Old Testament; the following quarter, a course in New Testament; and the third quarter, a course in Christian ethics. These three with a course in Comparative Religion, began a four-quarter cycle, that continues to this very day. In a state where prayers cannot be offered in public school classrooms, courses are offered with the New York State University credit in a community college for Old Testament, New Testament, Christian ethics, and comparative religion taught by qualified theologians and teachers.

"Knock, and it shall be opened unto you."

Knock that the doors to enlightenment may be opened in the educational institutions and processes of our time. Knock that barriers to misunderstanding and prejudice may be eliminated and destroyed. Knock that the walls of separation and segregation may come tumbling down, that openness and clarity may become the order of the day.

"Ask, and it shall be given you!

"Seek, and ye shall find!

"Knock, and it shall be opened unto you!"

The opportunities in our time are second to none in history. Never before have there been as many from whom we might ask, as broad horizons toward which we might seek, such noble causes for which we might knock.

It will be a tragic awakening if one day we stand at the gates of hell and hear One say: "It could have been heaven; but you did not ask, you would not seek, and you did not knock!"

"More and More or Less and Less"

"For unto every one that hath shall be given, and he shall have abundance: but from him that hath not shall be taken away even that which he hath."
—The Gospel According to Matthew 25:29

What would you do if you had a million dollars?

That possibility is not as remote today as it was a half-century ago. In my boyhood days, the Irish Sweepstakes offered that opportunity as one in a hundred million; but sweepstakes and lotteries in the United States have now become as common as apple pie.

A millionaire in the twenties was considered quite unusual, but today sportspersons with millions traipse across the diamonds, gridirons, courts, links, greens, and turfs. Most people consider wealthy, professional athletes as a matter of fact.

On afternoon talk shows some have shared their experience of how they made a million or lost a million—some in real estate, some in stocks and bonds, and some in short-term, high-risk investments.

Yes, you could be a millionaire! Well, maybe you would not have quite a million dollars, but you could well be among those having more and more instead of those having less and less.

How? There are almost as many ways of gaining this world's goods as there are people in the world; and strange as it may seem, the secret is found in the teachings of Jesus. Consider the Parable of the Talents.

The nobleman was going on an extensive journey, and being keenly aware of what he had and the value of life's gifts to him, he called in three of his hired servants and said to each, "Occupy until I come."

He gave five talents to one. He gave two talents to a second. He gave one talent to a third. Time passed, and the nobleman returned and required an accounting of their stewardship.

The one to whom five talents had been given gave an accounting of his stewardship with great enthusiasm. "Lord, thou deliveredst unto me five talents: behold, I have gained beside them five talents more."

The one to whom two talents had been given gave an accounting of his stewardship with equally great joy. "Lord, thou deliveredst unto me two talents: behold, I have gained two other talents beside them."

The one to whom one talent had been given gave an accounting of his stewardship, and in all seriousness said: "Lord, I knew thee that thou art an hard man, reaping where thou hast not sown, and gathering where thou hast not strawed: And I was afraid, and went and hid my talent in the earth: lo, there thou hast that is thine."

Many in our society considering the teachings of Jesus and providing a conclusion to the story would say: Too bad. Here is an unfortunate person. We will take some from the person who gained five talents, and some from the person who gained two talents, and we will make certain that all three servants have the same.

But this is not the way the story ends! Instead of taking talents from those who had five, plus five, and two plus two, he takes the talent from the one who had only one talent, much to the surprise of almost every one, and gives it to the person who had gained the most. Indeed the story of Jesus is a story of two who gained more and more and one who received less and less.

This, is the way it was in the beginning, this is the way it is now, and this is the way it will be in the future.

This is a story of Jesus, a parable, if you please, a Christian fact of life.

So you want to have a million dollars. You want to be among those who have more and more instead of among those who have less and less. What do you do? Even if you are to marry a millionaire, it will require a first step.

A Leap of Faith

In the story of these three servants there was no fear in the mind of the one to whom five talents were given, nor in the mind of the one to whom two talents were given. Only in the third was there fear. Openly, without mental reservation or a moment's hesitation, he said, "I was afraid."

Fear has no place on the diamonds, gridirons, or courts. Fear has no place on the links, the greens, or the turf. Topps Chewing Gum's Hall of Fame has no pictures of folk who are afraid. There are no portraits either of folk who experienced faith without reason.

Now one cannot exercise faith without reason. Confidence to win a place depends on the ability to run, good feet, and sound legs. Confidence to sing well depends on good lungs, breath control, and a pleasing voice.

Certainly each can be improved, but there has to be evidence of certain and reasonable potential before there can be a responsible beginning.

The leap of faith must begin where you are, with what you have, and in line with that which God has given you. Consistency is an important ingredient in the story that Jesus told. The one who had five talents gained five talents because he had faith that he was capable of gaining five more. The one who had two talents gained two talents because he had faith that he was capable of gaining two more. The quantitative worth is not the point. Here was faith and here was gain consistent with conviction. The end result was complementary to a leap of faith.

This brings us to the second element in the parable of Jesus. If you want to be among those who have more and more instead of among those who have less and less, even if you were to marry a millionaire, you must complement the leap of faith with hope.

A Focus on Hope

Primitive man attempting to light his first fire anticipated sparks from the striking flint stones. If there had been no hope for a spark there would never have been reason to strike the stones together. Primitive man hoped for a spark. With joyful expectation he struck the flint stones together. With glee he saw the spark ignite a flame—and that spelled progress.

The servant who had five talents had his eye on five talents more. He hoped for them. Hope placed them in the grasp of the possible.

The servant with two talents had his eye on two talents more. He hoped for them. Hope placed them in the grasp of the possible.

The servant with the one talent had his eye only on that one talent. That is all that he had hoped for, and that was all he had when the appointed time came. Because that was all he had, he was fearful of losing it, even that one talent was taken from him. A tragedy indeed—a life without a dream.

In the parable of the talents, Jesus does not speak of the milestones of progress, but you can rest assured that they were there. While the long-term goal for the one with five talents seeking five talents more was ten talents, you may be sure that the path was marked for the sixth, the seventh, the eighth, and the ninth talent as well. And along the way there was a season and a reason for rejoicing because the lesser goals were attained one by one.

While the long-term goal for the one with two talents seeking two talents more was four talents, his path also was marked for the third as well as the fourth talent, and along the way he too rejoiced as the lesser goal was attained.

Life and time require of us the setting of the lesser goals as well as the greater goal. If time runs out before the greater goal is reached, there is cause for rejoicing for the attainment of the lesser goals along the way. Each goal, in fact, is a blessing. A gospel songwriter emphasizes the importance of each by expressing it in these words: "Count your many blessings, name them one by one."

In the far distance we see the goal through hopeful eyes, and lesser goals along the way; and as each of our expectations is met, there is joy. But the story told by Jesus does not end there.

Accountability and Reward

Each of the three servants was called upon to give an accounting of themselves. The one to whom five talents were given had obtained five talents more, and he reported on that progress. The one to whom two talents were given had attained two talents more, and he reported on that progress. The one to whom one talent was given reported his plight: an unchanged value limited by fear. Because of fearfulness and hopelessness, he was deprived of even the one talent he had had.

The one who had five talents gained five talents more, and behold he was given an extra one. Progress? Indeed! His course was from five talents to ten talents, to eleven talents in all. Good reason for rejoicing. The goal was attained. He had given a good accounting. He had gained a reward.

A five-talent man named Paul put it in these words: "I have fought a good fight, I have finished my course, I have kept the faith: Henceforth there is laid up for me a crown of righteousness, which the Lord, the righteous judge, shall give me at that day: and not to me only, but unto all them also that love his appearing" (2 Timothy 4:7-8).

What does this mean for you? For me?

It means that each of us has the choice of living among those with more and more or with less and less. How amazing that not only is the story true and the principle sound, but that we have a choice. The choice is between more and more or less and less.

Take a leap of faith. Focus on hope. Prove accountability and receive a reward.

With these a five-talent man became an eleven-talent man, and his accomplishment is permanently engraved in history.

And, the best part of it all is that you can do it too.

Your Name Is Not
the Game

"And he called unto him his disciples, and saith unto them, Verily I say unto you, That this poor widow hath cast more in, than all they which have cast into the treasury: For all they did cast in of their abundance; but she of her want did cast in all that she had, even all her living."
—The Gospel According to Mark 12:43-44

What is a name?

We all consider our names to be important. We like to be known. We are greatly pleased if, upon meeting someone a second time that person is readily able to identify us and call us by name. And we are impressed even more when someone we perhaps have never met personally calls us by name the very first time we meet.

A former president of the Brown Shoe Company in Shenandoah, Iowa, was very popular in his area as an after dinner speaker. It was his custom to arrive at an event early, greet all guests as they arrived, and at the beginning of his address introduce everyone around the tables by name. It was an effective means of getting their attention for his subject, using his splendid gift for making friends. And believe me, he sold shoes! His addresses were not significant in and of themselves. But the impression he made was indelible. In fact, the impression spans more than thirty-five years of my own lifetime. I can see him as clearly as if he were present, because he remembered my name.

Paging through the Scriptures there are names that we can identify from childhood because of the lessons we learned in church school. Name a book in the Bible and certain names will come to mind for each of us:

> Genesis—Adam and Eve
> Exodus—Moses
> Judges—Sampson
> Ruth—Naomi
> Kings—David
> Job—Bildad and Eliphaz
> Esther—Mordecai
> Matthew—John the Baptist
> The Acts—Saul of Tarsus
> Philemon—Onesimus the Slave

But some of the most significant characters are those whose names are beyond recall. They are known not for what they were called, but they were known for what they did. Even the names that leaped from memory in associating persons with the books listed above were names of persons whose deeds gave them significnce. It was the life they lived, the work they did, the faith to which they gave expression in the course of their years. And in every book there are personalities which come to mind, their names known only to God, because they made a significant contribution to history. Your name is not the game! Life, as an expression of faith, is. In the course of your life, many will be guided, will receive direction, and will gain help by things you do, words you say, positions you assume—and they may never learn your name. Many nameless persons come to mind as we read the Gospels, and I would focus your attention on one such person now.

A Poor Widow

Think of anyone in the first century likely to be completely overlooked. A woman? Probably. A widow? Certainly.

Women in every age have been considered the weaker sex. In the first century a woman without a husband was deemed a person with no reason for being at all.

True, there are some women whose names come to mind as we read the Gospels, but most are identified more by relationship than by person. Let's look at some examples.

The Virgin Mary. She is known in history because she was the mother of our Lord. To many she was known as the wife of Joseph. To some, a foster mother to the beloved disciple John. But take from her the Christ event of Bethlehem, and you would probably never have known of her person or name.

Elizabeth. She is known in history because she was the mother of John the Baptist. To many she was known as the wife of Zechariah. To some she was known as the Aunt of Jesus of Nazareth. But take from her the birth of John the Baptist, and you would probably never have known of her person or name.

Mary Magdalene. She is known in history because she was a companion to Jesus. To many she was known as an adulteress. To some she was known as a soothsayer. But take from her the presence of the Teacher of Galilee, and you would probably never have heard of her person or name.

In biblical times women simply were not known because

they were women. If you think we are in a man's world today, think of the masculine complex in the first century. Society allowed women no rights. They had no privileges. They received few honors. They lived without respect. An average father would sell his daughter for almost any price. If there were any value in a woman's life at all, it would be measured by the male children she might conceive and bear and the quality of physical life that may come through her as it was presumed that she would carry a man's seed in her body. To be a woman was the bottom of the totem pole in first-century society.

However, there was one classification of even less distinction than this. That was to be a widow. A woman who had been married. A woman whose spouse had died. A woman who was cast out by both society and fate.

Seemingly independent, she was actually totally dependent upon others. Her lot was to beg for meager provisions in daily bread. If there was any hope at all for significance in life, it would be to become impregnated with the seed of a brother-in-law.

A woman, a widow and nameless. From a lowest of lowly positions in life, she leaps out of the pages of history with significance.

Religious Person

We catch a glimpse of the widow in Jerusalem at the Temple. It is the place of alms. Not the place where alms are being asked—on the outer porch, but actually at the place where alms are given, a sacred place of the Most High God.

A similar event took place in Indonesia a short time ago. A Christian worship service had just concluded, worship-

ers had greeted one another and parted with fond
farewells, and the minister was closing the sanctuary to
protect the contents from vandals and the place of worship
from adverse conditions in that climate. A little woman
came and insisted that she be given the privilege of
entering the church. She was told that the services had
ended, the worshipers had left. Nevertheless she earnestly
pleaded that she be permitted to enter the sanctuary as she
wanted to present her offering. Permission was granted;
and as she approached the Communion table, she untied
the hem of her sari and released a coin which she presented
as her offering.

When leaving the sanctuary, the woman looked down to
the carpet spotted with little drops of blood. She was
embarrassed by them; for in walking to the church, little
stones had pierced her tender feet, and the spots were the
result of these wounds. You see, she was a leper. Cast out
from society, but grateful for the encouragement of a loving
Savior, she came in her untouchable condition to present
her gift to God. Upon leaving the sanctuary, she said: "I'm
sorry. I simply had to give." She was a person of great
religious persuasion who was determined to give witness to
her faith.

We could list many reasons why these two women
should not have come, should not have given. Regardless of
what they may have had, life would give them but little
more. Regardless of the condition of their bodies, age
would never be on their side again. Regardless of the size of
their gift, large or small, the particular asset was not likely
to be replaced. Regardless of the need, there surely were
literally hundreds of people more capable of giving than
they.

While there was an urge to give, certainly for every need

there would be a hundred reasons not to give. While it was a tradition to give to the temple or church, there were good reasons to give to literally hundreds of other deserving causes. Needs and opportunities existed then even as they do now. But there was a credibility in the institution complementary to the Divine will which insisted, "This is the time. Here is the place."

Consider the choice by the widow in the gospel record, and evaluate that choice in terms of the time in which we live. Her gift was presented to, actually through, the temple. Consider the place of organized religion in the lives of people in those times. The religious organization provided few and certainly the only social services there were to meet the needs of the underprivileged, physically handicapped, mentally and emotionally disturbed people in those times. As an example folk, through conversion, soon discovered that they were alienated from the benevolent structure of their society when they became Christians. The need for members to have all things in common, to name deacons to provide food and services to widows and orphans, is obvious in the Acts of the Apostles. This need was evident because as Christians, they were divorced from the support means for humanitarian services in the religious structure of their times. This widow contributed her two mites to enable the temple staff to meet the spiritual, social, and physical needs of the society of which she was a part. No place in her tradition could she make an offering which could provide as great a service to the divine mission in time than through the temple.

While there is a multiplicity of organizations and agencies to serve the needs of particular people in today's society, the church stands significantly apart from each in that it fills the gap of unmet needs in the community structure; and where duplication of services seems to persist, there is a uniqueness in that service that is up and beyond that offered by other agencies. Here, too, there is no place where an offering, a gift, may provide as great a service to the divine mission in time than through the church.

These facts were readily recognized by both the widow at the temple and the Teacher from Nazareth. Their minds were synchronized to this event. With a religious orientation and a posture of sanctifying grace, she did that which would be considered good, not only in her own mind, but in the mind of God and in the minds of the people. After all, she was a religious person. Through this act of grace she became known in history.

An Immortal Personality

An anonymous poet put it in these words:

> I'm writing a Gospel, a chapter each day,
> Through the things I do, the words I say.
> Men will not read the message true
> So what is the Gospel according to you?

James emphasizes the fact that persons are known by their works, by the things they do. Some assume that they will be remembered by their speaking, by saying much. But immortality is gained through what one does.

On the northern shore of Manhattan Island, there is a place called Hudson's Cove. Henry Hudson's ship anchored there. It was in that place that he traded with the Indians, and it was there that he made an indelible impression on them of the importance of European traders, their goods, and the presence of pioneer settlers. Nothing noted there is of what he said. The place will be significant through the whole of our nation's history because of what he did.

In eastern Pennsylvania there is a battleground of some significance in the history of this republic. A President of the United States was invited to speak in commentary on the struggle and suffering of those who bled and died on those sacred grounds. One may travel up and down the coast from the James River to New England and note historical markers distinguishing the place of important contests in the struggle for freedom. But Abraham Lincoln caused Gettysburg to gain special significance because of the battle, his presence, and an address of such brevity that those who heard it would not applaud. As a result, this event is remembered by almost every United States citizen and has become a part of their knowledge of the nation's history.

In New England there is a school which was opened for female students, because the founder had a keen awareness of the capability of women students and a firm conviction in the equality of the sexes. One cannot read of her life without being in awe of her great determination in overcoming the obstacles that were placed in her way—obstacles which today seem far fetched and unreasonable, beyond the threshold of a civilized people. But they occurred. And the determination of the pioneer in education for women prevailed. The name of Emma Hart Willard is immortal because of what she did in creating a new day for womanhood in the whole of history.

The name is not the game. The game is what you do and the significant contribution that you make through your life and work. Consider again this woman to whom Jesus calls our attention. She was a widow, an outcast, seemingly a nobody. But she invested the whole of her living in a charitable event, and there is likely not a Christian on the face of the earth that does not remember her. Thank God for the contribution that she has made to both your life and mine.

The impact that you make on the lives of others by the things you do, the evidence of the things you believe, will make a far more lasting impression on people than the engraved letters on stone that will mark the place where you rest, your name and the dates of your birth and death.

The widow at the Temple impresses us with the fact that the name is not the game, for the game is life and the stewardship you exercise over it.

A Case Against Logic

"Give, and it shall be given unto you; good measure, pressed down, and shaken together, and running over, shall men give into your bosom. For with the same measure that ye mete withal it shall be measured to you again."
—The Gospel According to Luke 6:38

Although I was raised in a family of modest means, the admonition to save for a rainy day was reverenced and exercised in our daily lives. While the family budget was too limited to provide a weekly allowance, our labor in simple chores or exhaustive work was rewarded to a degree consistent with the family's wherewithal. Actually, the most generous employers were those beyond the family circle, and while the chores were frequently the same, it always seemed less burdensome and more interesting if they were across the street, down the block, or on the other side of town.

While, as boys, we earned the money, our parents were the comptrollers, and few requisitions reached sales persons without their perusing them and approving them. Our tendency always was to spend now. Their counsel almost always was to wait. We were inclined to buy cheap products of little or no worth. They were inclined to encourage us to wait until we could spend more and secure quality merchandise. Often, when our decisions prevailed and merchandise of lesser value and good proved inadequate for our needs, and disappointment became a product of our way, there was the usual reminder that you cannot have your cake and eat it too. The more you spend, the less you are going to have. No one had to venture far into the economic order of things to be convinced of this truth. Experience soon proved the validity of the thesis. It was true beyond the shadow of a doubt. It is simple logic: The more you spend the less you will have.

I have traveled through all fifty of our states and to forty-seven countries of the world. I have dealt in forty-eight different currencies. Whether we dealt in rubles, francs, or pounds; gilders, yen or dollars, the fact remained: the more we spent, the less we had. Whether we visit a kindergarten or nursing home, a dimestore or a bank, no one will question the validity of the thesis. No one can save that which they spend. The more you spend, the less you will have. It is a simple truth about money.

However, if we turn to the Gospels, we discover a case against logic. Logic tells us that the more we spend the less we will have, and it is true whether we spend our money for food or for clothing, for shelter or for transportation, for furniture or for equipment. A dollar spent, in a sense, is a dollar lost! It doesn't take a very strong case to convince anyone of this fact. But Jesus confronts us with a case against logic. He says, "The more you give, the more you will receive." The greater your benevolence, the greater your capability to be benevolent. The more philanthropic you are, the more philanthropic you can be.

"Give and it will be given unto you!"

The Case Against Logic as a Life-style

In all of life there is nothing as repulsive as a selfish or self-centered person. As we move through the several stages of life, they are noticed along the way. They are not appreciated by their peers, they are not respected among their colleagues, and they are not considered warmly by their neighbors. However, they are not entirely without reward. They appreciate, respect, and honor themselves.

Jesus had much to say concerning a professional religious group in the primitive Christian period. Of all the people of that time, no group received as much of his anger as they did. Paul alluded to them as a sect. He was a product of their schooling. They were known as the Pharisees.

Our Lord speaks of two men who went up to the temple to pray. One was a Pharisee and the other was a publican. The publican, in a rather sheltered and remote corner of the temple, prayed in solitude, "Lord, be merciful to me a sinner." The Pharisee, to the contrary, in the busy thoroughfare of the nave, assumed a conspicuous pose and prayed, "Lord, I thank Thee that I am not as other men." His life-style was obvious to all: "Look at me. I'm good. I'm better than anyone else."

The Master stated that the Pharisee had his reward: self-esteem today, but little hope for a brighter tomorrow.

Consider, if you will, those who emboss the fabric of your acquaintance with a life-style like that:

They love to be seen. They want to be heard. They are determined to be known. Their motive and process are at the expense of all others. They have nothing to give. They can only receive. Their life is nothing more than a noisy gong or a clanging cymbal.

Destiny brings them to loneliness, separateness, and emptiness. Rich, perhaps—but poor. Impoverished from the splendor of fulfillment and the living of a life truly worthwhile.

This is a case against logic as a life-style.

The Case Against Logic as an Example of Good

In the course of Christian perspective, we have been strong in the emphasis of a poverty-stricken Christ. One hymn-writer put it in these words: "My Master was so very poor." We glean through the Gospels and seemingly reap supportive documentation all along the way. He was born in a stable. He was cradled in a manger. He was without a pillow upon which to lay his head. In death, he was placed in another man's tomb.

I am thoroughly convinced that we have misinterpreted the evidence of history. We have misinterpreted the evidence of history when we overlook the fact that he was of the house and lineage of David—a person of noble birth. We have misinterpreted the evidence of history when we overlook the fact that Mary and Joseph proceeded first to the inn and were excluded, it was not because they were without the means to stay there, but because the inn was without adequate rooms to care for the guests who sought shelter there. We have misinterpreted the evidence of history when we overlook the fact that the Holy Family were honored guests at a wedding in Cana, the Master a welcome friend in a home in Bethany, and the Healer a sought-out physician by even a centurion of his time. Are these the credentials of a hermit, a wanderer, a person without substance? Certainly not!

We have misinterpreted the evidence of history when we overlook the fact that the Master sent his disciples ahead to Jerusalem in order that they might secure a place for the celebration of the Passover—the first Lord's Supper. There is no evidence to assume that they were without means, seeking free accomodations, just any shelter from a storm. They fulfilled their assignment by arranging for an adequate, commodious upper room.

We have misinterpreted the evidence of history if we climb the hill called Calvary and fail to see the robe he wore—one of so fine a quality and great a value that the cloth should not be cut. Dice were cast for the prize, and the winner considered fortunate.

Follow carefully the career of the Nazarene, and you will discover one who gave little or no thought to himself. His was a life devoted to meeting the needs of others. At Cana of Galilee, it was a determination to provide adequate wine for a time of celebration when the supply proved inadequate. At the family residence in Bethany it was the zeal to ensure life in an experience of hopelessness at the brink of death. For the centurion's servant it was a determination that the one diseased and ravished with pain might be made whole again. How could one be so foolish as to call that poverty? Was it really poverty or was it the impoverishment of self through self-giving?

In the life and teachings of Jesus, consideration of the problems and needs of others was of primary importance. If one were in need of a coat, that may or may not in itself be adequate, one is to be willing to give not only the coat but a cloak also. If a burden could be lightened by assisting a person over the space of a mile, it was not only good to do so, but it was even better when one were willing to go even a second mile. If one were at wit's end and incensed against you to the extent that that person would strike you upon the cheek, be open to help them give full vent to their anger by turning to them still the other cheek.

Startling is the command of Jesus that if one were to borrow from you, lend to that person according to his need;

and at the same time, deep down in your heart, hope that it will not be repaid to you again.

In the parable of the pounds, one having ten pounds made another ten pounds and was given an additional one by his master because he exercised good stewardship over the talents originally given to him. And what does the Lord require of us? To do good, to love mercy, and to walk humbly with God.

This is a case against logic as an example of good.

The Case Against Logic as a Generous Person

"Give and it shall be given unto you."

How much? It would seem reasonable if the assurance were only to replenish that which was given. If you give a dollar, you will receive a dollar. If you give a coat, you will receive a coat. If you give a meal, you will receive a meal. But the Christian promise goes beyond this.

Hear the Word of the Lord: "Give and it shall be given to you. Good measure. Pressed down. Shaken together. Running over."

In the travels of Paul there were areas where he was received with much enthusiasm and with great hospitality. There were also the areas where there was keen opposition and seemingly a lack of appreciation for his ministry and talent.

Except for the offerings taken for the saints in Jerusalem, he took nothing from any community in which he served. While he insisted that the laborer was worthy of his hire, he was determined that his personal advancement would never be at the expense of others. Yet resources ever poured into his life, so much so in fact that he could assure the Corinthians, "God is able to make all grace abound toward you; that ye, always having all sufficiency in all things, may abound to every good work" (2 Corinthians 9:8). Think of the significance of that witness in a society where we are determined to get all that we can regardless of the method or circumstances. Here is the secret to what many need to experience most in the Christian life: Give and it shall be given unto you.

As a life-style, as an example of good, as a generous person it goes against all logic—but it is Christian truth.

The Verdict Is Yours

"And the King shall answer and say unto them, Verily I say unto you, Inasmuch as ye have done it unto one of the least of these my brethen, ye have done it unto me."
—The Gospel According to Matthew 25:40

Judgment is one of the thorny issues in theological dialogue as various denominations and sects of Christianity endeavor to move toward church unity. It was a thorny issue when the monk Martin Luther challenged the right of Rome to sell indulgences, and it is a thorny issue today as penitents wrestle with decisions for private confession in a booth or corporate confession in a service of public worship.

The complexity of the issue of judgment is not limited to indulgences or public vs. private confession. The type and degree go to extremes with numerous positions at literally hundreds of points of difference in between.

The Matter of Judgment

There is the position of the judgmentalist who wants all to stand before a great white throne and be examined for all that has been done in each lifetime. The evaluation is to be precise, meticulous, and fair. The compensatory factor extreme to the n'th degree. "Be sure your sins will find you out. . . . That which is done in secret will be shouted from the housetops. . . . There will be weeping and gnashing of teeth." I was nurtured in this kind of theology.

There are also the libertines who insist that we have all been freed from sin and death through the suffering of our Lord and Savior, Jesus Christ, on the cross. There is therefore no judgment, and without judgment, there can be no condemnation; and with no condemnation, there can be no death. "The law of the spirit of life in Christ has delivered us from the law of sin and death." Strange as it may seem, I was nurtured on this kind of theology as well.

Both theological concepts were often evident in the same religious grouping with exegesis and exposition as products of a single minister. It depended on chapter and verse. It depended on the season in the Christian year. It depended on the text for the day. There apparently was no need for consistency. Passages and texts were selected to accomodate the pastor's understanding of the situation and the mode that would best serve his purposes in ministry to the particular congregation at a particular time.

The longest single dissertation of the Master recorded in the Gospels is on judgment. It is reported in Matthew 25. The judgment is comprehensive—it includes all nations. It is specific—it weighs each individual deed. It is diverse and divisive—for some it provides entrance into a kingdom prepared from the beginning of time, and for others, expulsion to everlasting punishment. Certainly this takes no Christian by surprise. With inequities and iniquities throughout the whole of life, we tend to believe that there must be a day of reckoning someplace, somehow. Jesus affirms that there is. Many find comfort in this.

The Criteria for Judgment

While there is little or no element of surprise in the fact that there is judgment, there is an element of surprise in the criteria for approval and acceptability in the divine plan. In fact, Jesus is very clear in stating that the verdict is yours. There are no circumstances beyond your control. You have the key. The decision is in your hands.

In computing what a sentence should be, most were using the indices provided by their ecclesiastical structures. Times for worship, study, and prayer were considered to be of great importance and were weighed heavily on the scale of justice. But we face a shocking experience if some of those who worshiped, studied, and prayed are identified among those to be cursed, and some of those who have not worshiped, studied, and prayed are praised and blessed.

In the teachings of Jesus, the focus for worthiness was taken from the altar to the street, the sanctuary to the prison, the choirloft and the pulpit to the highways and the byways of life. The emphasis was changed entirely from a focus on those who had the finest of vestments literally to those who had none.

To those upon the right hand, the Son of man says, "Come! Enter! The Kingdom has been prepared for you from the foundation of the earth." We've been waiting for you for a long, long time.

I was hungry and you fed me. You saw to it that I had food.

I was thirsty and you gave me drink. You saw to it that I had water.

I was a stranger and you took me in. You did not leave me alone and lonely.

I was naked and you clothed me. You saw to it that I had clothes.

I was sick and you visited me. You showed deep concern for each of my hurts.

I was in prison and you came to me. You continued to be my friend.

Viewing the Son of man, those on the right hand were taken completely by surprise." Certainly they had been with folk of these circumstances along the way, but never had they seen Jesus. At times the folk were black, white, yellow, brown, or red. At times they were young, and at times they were old. At times they were men and boys, and at times women and girls. Never the Nazarene!

"We did for others. Never for you!" This was their common reply. The response of Jesus was simple and clear, "Inasmuch as ye did it unto one of the least of these my brethren, ye did it unto me."

To those on the left hand the Son of man says:

"Depart from me ye cursed! You deserve to be punished always! There is no room for you here!

I was hungry and you were not concerned. I was thirsty and you did not care. I was a stranger and you shut me out of your life. I was naked and you made sport of my condition. I was sick and my chills, and my fever, and my hurts did not penetrate your consciousness. I was in prison and you refused to identify with me in my plight."

Viewing the Son of man, those on the left hand, too, were taken by surprise. Certainly there had been folk of circumstances much as these along the way, but never had they seen Jesus. The people were black, white, yellow, brown, or red. There were the old, the middle-aged, the young. There were men and boys, there were women and girls. Never the Nazarene.

"We did not do it for others—but we would have done it for you." A likely response. The words of Jesus as a result of a review of these facts were simply these: "Inasmuch as ye did not do it unto one of the least of these my brethren, ye did not do it unto me!"

Now we assume that this is certainly not a dissertation that applies to us in our day and age. The population of the world is so great, human needs so persistent, transgressions so numerous that the story simply cannot apply to us. After all, we all do some good. While we do not give much, we do give some. Almost everyone is helped by what we do.

Almost everyone? Helped? Really?

Focus your mind on these again:

The hungry.

The thirsty.

The stranger.

The inadequately clothed.

The ill.

The imprisoned.

Almost everyone is helped by what we do. Practically no one, in fact few indeed, is really helped by what we do. Which statement would truly be the most correct?

"We sent our check." "We gave at the office." "We support our own church." But when we consider the "freight," the administrative cost, how much did we really give? The envelope and the postage? The receipt and the accounting processes? The organization's investment in development to sustain and perhaps increase our gifts the second, third and fourth time around?

Determining the Verdict

How much did you say you gave? Accounting processes are costly. If your gift did not exceed seven dollars, you gave nothing more than the cost of processing your gift. If the organization responded with a personal letter, a five dollar contribution may have left them seven dollars in the hole! The truth of the matter is that the hungry are not being fed, the thirsty do not have their thirst assuaged, the strangers continue to be strangers, the naked are not being clothed, the ill are not being healed, and those in prison are bankrupt of hope simply because we do not give wisely and our giving does not make a difference. Many of our processes result in the have's having more and some who have not having less. In this sermon of Jesus, it is interesting that we focus on particular needs. Not that we focus on impoverishment in the human family generally, but that we focus on specific needs, individual situations, and those in want of special care.

We spend a lot on providing foodstuffs to the hungry, but a problem assumed to have attained a solution at noontime feels the pangs of hunger at the beginning of another day.

We spend a lot to provide water for those who are thirsty, but the tap is turned off if they cannot pay the water bill.

We spend a lot on providing services for strangers, and we delegate responsibilty for their care to those who will be certain to keep them out of our way.

We spend a lot to provide clothing for folk who are cold or whose bodies blister from the sun, but the cold and heat simply will not go away, and the law of averages satisfies our conscience, but it does not eliminate basic human need when the garments are old and worn.

We spend a lot on hospitals, doctors, nurses, and nursing care; but they are directed primarily to those who can, through some kind of insuring process, pay their own way.

We spend a lot on prisons and prisoners, and we tend to

call the process rehabilitation but few, if any, are rehabilitated along the way.

This dissertation of Jesus insists that it is time for us to do something. Not a time to give little, but a time to give much!

Two illustrations from the life of our Blessed Lord come to my mind. One focuses on a widow and the other on a little boy. We do not know their names, they are not important. The illustrations, however, dolly in on a single event in each of their lives.

The widow presents her mite as her contribution to the redemptive processes of her times. She gives all of her living! Jesus calls our attention to that fact. The little boy presents his basket of goods consisting of five loaves and two fish. He gives all that he has. Jesus also calls our attention to that fact.

But the Master did not stop with these. He was not content to merely use illustrations or to point to his contemporaries. Female or male, old or young. He could attain his purpose only with the complete gift of himself—His very life, all that he had, all that he was, and all that he could ever hope to be. Calvary made the difference.

The task before us is not merely to share, to give modestly, or even to give proportionately. The task before us is to be generous, to be gracious, and to be considerate. The task before us is to bring to complete resolution the problems of human need, human deprivation, and human suffering in the world today.

The righteous were embraced and blessed by God because human needs were met, problems were solved, and society was made whole again. Those who had been hungry had food. Those who had been thirsty had water to drink. Those who had felt strange had a sense of belonging. Those who had been naked had clothing to wear. Those who had been sick knew the warmth and concern of loving care. Those who had been imprisoned became one in the family of man again.

Considering the world of need, the potential for good in that which you have—the very wealth of your life—what verdict will you implant in the Master's mind for yourself?

Your Right to Share

"And Jesus sat over against the treasury, and beheld how
the people cast money into the treasury."
—The Gospel According to Mark 12:41

The church tends to be an exclusive organization. In
some places it excludes blacks, and in some places it
excludes whites. In some places it excludes the young, and
in some places it excludes the old. In some places it
excludes townspeople, and in some places it excludes
country folk. The church has even been known, in some
cases, to exclude the rich and in other places to exclude the
poor. No church claiming the name of Christ has the right
to exclude anyone. And in the area of finance, Jesus is clear
in saying: "You belong! You have a right to share!"

The Approval for Giving

In theological circles little consideration is given to
stewardship inasmuch as both money and property are
considered to be unclean. Christianity has been overly
impressed by the fact that Jesus had no place to lay his
head, risked the payment of taxes on a disciple catching a
fish with a coin in its mouth, and openly rebuked a Pharisee
with wealth. Few seem knowledgeable of the fact that

Jesus' coat was considered to be of great worth, and the tomb selected for his body was one that was impressive and indicative of wealth.

Jesus, in the Gospel of Mark, is seen seated by the treasury. Here, at the temple, people were presenting their offerings. It was probably not a sabbath day. They were not sharing in a service of worship. Plates or baskets were not being circulated among the crowds inviting, or begging, for people to share. Out of convenience, and out of conviction, they brought their gifts.

It is obvious that Jesus approved. While he observed the many who contributed, he had criticism for none. Actually there was praise and approval of those who contributed from their living, their resources for God's work in time. In this event they were involved in the process of giving money. For some it may have been more convenient to give produce, for some livestock, and for some products from the work of their hands. In this event, and in this place, the support means for God's work was the coin of the realm.

Many in our churches would be critical of this today. It was not an act of worship. It was not a part of a religious service. There was not a collecting or offering process. There was no liturgy, apparently no prayer of dedication or even a priest standing by to express gratitude or to pronounce a blessing. It appeared to be a cold, irrelevant, and irreverent process.

It is strange to many that Jesus did not object to a lack of ritual and liturgy. They assume that Jesus observing such a process would have chosen to stand in their way, rebuke them and drive them, along with the money changers, out of the temple. Rather than disapprove, Jesus approved. He expressed no criticism of those who shared in ministry and mission in this way. They were engaging in an accepted process. Jesus approved of giving.

Today new modes of funding the church are being introduced. A few years ago, an Automatic Commitment Transfer Service was introduced to churches in pilot areas across the United States, and many objected strenuously. It is a process which provides financial support through automatic debits against checking and bank-card accounts. Automatically funds are programmed to move from the accounts of donors to the accounts of churches and church-related agencies at a particular time each month. Criticisms focused on sacred concerns. These concerns were not restricted to the clergy. They were concerns of many whose religious orientation was programmed entirely to the known and accepted practices of the church as used over the past fifty years. In these, people are restricted concerning giving:

Giving must be on Sunday.

It must be a part of worship.

It must be in church.

They are uncomfortable about the state of the church, and the future of the church, as life-styles become secular and cashless. They are concerned when folk are absent from church for three-day weekends, and holy days become holidays. The tendency is to condemn. They are concerned when folk miss the support process for a week or a month. By and large they are unwilling to recognize change in life-styles and reprogram the church in terms of times of worship or other means of financial support more appropriate to their fiscal processes. Rather, they condemn. In this event of Scripture, they would be much more comfortable if Jesus were openly to disapprove of the process. It would be better for them if Jesus had said: "This is not the time. This is not the place. This is not the way." In opposition to their preferences, Jesus approves. The people are giving. The people have a right to give. Jesus approves of giving!

As we become increasingly involved in computer processing whereby the transfer of funds is automatically accomplished through touch-button telephones, through preauthorized payments against checking and bank card accounts, we need to know that our Lord approves of giving. The instrument by which he may very well have stood if this Gospel account were to take place today, may very well be an electronic teller located in the narthex of a church, thereby funding the church's mission with more adequate resources to provide liberty to the captives as well as clothing and food for impoverished people. The church must ensure your right to give and provide the instrumentation for giving which will best accomodate your personal fiscal processes in responding to God's call to the greatest measure of your personal capability and the depth of your commitment. You have the right to give!

In considering those who came to the treasury with their financial support, Jesus notes two kinds of persons—those who gave of their abundance and those who gave from meager resources. And he has something significant to say of each. Let us consider them in the order of his observation.

Many Who Were Rich

The first-century world was in many respects similar to ours except for the fact that the percentages of the rich and poor were somewhat different from our situation today. There were fewer rich people and more poor people, percentagewise, in society then than there are today, and if there was a middle-income class, it was a group of such little significance that it was hardly known. There were a few of great wealth. There were many of little or no means. There were few in between.

It would seem likely in a society plagued by impoverishment that, perhaps, those of means, only a very few would come. But notice the words in the Gospel record: "Many that were rich cast in much." They that were rich came. They were many in number. They gave.

The record includes a fact not readily understood or accepted by an average person in the church today. We prefer to believe that the rich are rich because they are selfish and live with little or no concern for matters of faith and philanthropic service. But the record is clear. There can be no question. There is no room for argument. Many came.

A second observation recorded in the text is that out of their abundance, they gave much. They had an abundance. They gave much. The descriptive language is consistent. It is not as though they gave much from little means or gave little from great means. They had wealth. Their generosity was consistent with their means. They gave much!

Note the attitude of many toward the wealthy as they relate to the church. Some actually question the legitimacy of their membership in the household of faith. When we observe wealthy people attending church services, we inadvertently tend to think of the words of Jesus when he said, "It is easier for a camel to go through the eye of a needle, than for a rich man to enter into the kingdom of God" (Mark 10:25). And, the needle we use in our imagery is the needle in the sewing basket in our home. Regardless of the size of that needle we conclude that it is an impossible feat. But it was not impossible then and it is not impossible now. For the eye of the needle was a crevice in the passageway between the winter and summer pastures of Judea, where shepherds guided their flocks in a semiannual pilgrimage. It was not difficult for the shepherd, and it was easy for the sheep, to pass through the passage. It was difficult for the camel. In most cases the camels had to be relieved of their load and pass through the needle unencumbered. It took time. It took patience. It took care. But it was done, and Jesus did not imply that it was an impossibility.

The rich have a right to give. Each has a right to share. Jesus observed that out of their abundance they gave much. Much was needed then and much is needed now.

So often in the church we rejoice over such processes as the "fellowship of the least coin." We seem to believe that pennies dropping for Jesus are indeed feeding the hungry, clothing the poor, making literate the ignorant, and bringing to salvation those who do not have a vital understanding of Jesus Christ. But in many cases one person is matching the giving of those in a single congregation. In some cases, one person is giving more than the churches in an entire community. In few cases, one person is giving more than a single denomination. The church's mission is dependent upon that. As difficult as it is for the church to sustain mission in times of inflation and limited resources, thank God that folk of means are giving generously out of their abundance!

They have a right to give! They had a right to share in the time of our Blessed Lord, and they have a right to share now. As members of the household of faith, they belong. They are entitled to our respect. They are entitled to our concern. They are entitled to fellowship in the community of believers.

A Person of Modest Means

After considering those who gave much out of their abundance, Jesus focuses our attention on a second group, identified through a poor widow. A widow gave of her want and threw into the treasury two mites. They were worth a farthing. Today she may have given two nickels; they would be worth a dime.

Across the church she stands in distinction. She gave of her limited resources. In spite of her impoverishment, she wanted to give. She had a right to share.

How often in the church we give little thought to these folk and their need for the privilege of sharing. At times, in an every-member visitation when long-term commitments are sought for mission, we tend to write them off. Their support is not worth going after. It takes more gasoline than it is worth. Many have said: "I'll give five dollars more myself and save the time and trouble." But the less fortunate have a right to give! They have a right to share!

Isn't it strange? So often we delight in the processes that amplify the merit of one who gave little. We misuse it by asking a penny a meal in a war against hunger. We misuse it by celebrating the fellowship of the last coin in giving pennies when we ought to give dollars. We misuse it as we, out of our abundance, are content to give little.

Jesus did not include in his observation those who had much, giving little into the treasury. If he had, he most certainly would have called it the sacrifice of fools. Certainly the process would have been repulsive to his taste. Sharp and articulate would have been his criticism, striking at the very heart of those flaunting their coins of meager support from lives couched in plenty. On occasion, with open rebuke, I have been pained at the silliness and the dishonesty of sharing coins when the task of Christian discipleship requires much more. In such events we comfort ourselves by saying, "We're doing what the poor widow did."

We need to recognize the fact that we are not doing what the poor widow did until we give our all. We must become a part of the philanthropic process. Even folk of modest means have a right to share, and they have a right to give of that which they have. Jesus emphasized that: They have a right to give!

The Christian enterprise requires the dedication and support of every individual. The means of support must be broad enough to accommodate each life-style of fiscal process. We must accommodate those who may give out of their abundance and those who will share from their want. We must accommodate those who find it more acceptable to give through preauthorized commitments processed in their banking institutions and those who prefer to support through pocket money in the offertory processes. In each event, and in each process, there is a measure of self; and we will measure to God's full expectancy when we, out of plenty as out of want, give our all.

Salvation Now!

"And Jesus said unto him, This day is salvation come to thine house."
—The Gospel According to Luke 19:9

As we page through the Gospels, we cannot help but be impressed by those whose experience interwove with that of the Master. Some were old and some were young. Some were men and some were women. Some were boys and some were girls. Some were sickly and some were well. Some were rich and some were poor. Some were nameless and some were identified by both name and vocation. Zacchaeus is one such person.

While there are many things which we do not know about Zacchaeus, there are some things which we do know about him. We know that he was short in stature. We know that he was energetic, capable of climbing trees. We know that he was a chief among the publicans or tax collectors. We know that he was rich. We know that he was a Christian.

But these descriptions are much too brief for an identification of a person and a complete understanding of their place in Scripture.

Consider the Man

His name was Zacchaeus, and he lived in Jericho. Professionally he had subscribed to the supremacy of

Rome and had accepted as fact that that empire was sovereign over the Palestinian world. Having accepted that fact, he had assumed a position with the government and was considered a man of integrity, reliability, and trust. Likely, he began this occupation as a tax collector with modest responsibility, and as he proved capable he ascended through the ranks with greater responsibility until he became the chief of the publicans. It was a position that paid well. It placed one in a position of economic advantage. Through it one could gain affluence and influence. Yet, it was a position with social limitations.

In a sense, those Jews who worked for the government, and were approved by the government, became separated from the local population. They were important to those in government but were never accepted as their equals. They were important to those in the community but were never accepted as ordinary citizens. The Romans considered them a necessary evil, responsible for a task they simply could not do. The Judeans acknowledged them as necessary to government, but presumed them as betraying their nation. They were a part of Rome—but they did not belong. A part of Judea—but they were not accepted.

What caused such a man to assume such a role? One cannot be sure. But considering his physical stature, we may have a reason. He was a short person. Certainly through his growing years, he was embarrassed by his size. They may have called him "runt," "punk," or "shorty." Short legs would not permit him to move as fast as others or hurdle rocks, fences, or limbs. When it came to lifting loads, many would appear much stronger. When it came to seeing things, he would often have to rely on the descriptions of others. How could one compensate for such a limitation, almost a hardship?

There were a number of ways. Zacchaeus chose a vocation in government—a uniform, a badge, the prestige of office—a position that would elevate him above folk twice his size. He had Rome to back him up. Rome was on his side. Like it or not, he demanded respect that limited size could never provide, and those who were tall were made to look like midgets before him, and those who were big were made to appear small before him. He, as a publican, was made great; and the importance of his office made him one of the greater among the great, even a chief publican.

Commensurate with his occupation was his home. It was impressive. It was in keeping with his economic station. It was set aside from the housing for the Romans, for, after all, he was a Jew. It was set aside from the housing for the Jews, for, after all, he was a partner with Rome. A desirable home in an undesirable political climate. A desirable home in an undesirable social climate. Lacking fellowship with others in government and community, Zacchaeus and his family must have been rich in association with each other. Love for spouse. Love for children. Love for parents. Families under persecution have always been known as families with close association and deep commitment to one another. Zacchaeus was in such a situation. His immediate environment was one of love and appreciation. Rome provided respect and trust. Judea provided caution and suspicion. But no one can have all things, and love. Deep appreciation among family members may be as much as anyone can expect in this life. This was the story of the man Zacchaeus.

Consider the Place

Jesus of Nazareth, the teacher from Galilee, had come to town. He was well known. His reputation preceded him everywhere he went. Not only was there incentive to hear the man, there was incentive to see the man as well—the interesting things which he might do, the miracles he might perform.

Jesus was a great storyteller. His stories had been repeated from village to village. Some came from the lives of individuals and families. Some came from the workaday world as they related to towns, countryside, and sea. Some came from the elements as they focused on seeds, bushes, and trees. Some came from vocations, and the shepherds knew their worth as did those who tended vineyards, those who tilled the soil, and those who sailed the sea.

There was strong incentive to see Jesus. Not as much for his appearance but for what he would do. Page through the Gospels and you will note many deeds of great significance:

He cast out a devil.

He reduced a fever.

He eliminated a condition of palsy.

He stopped an issue of blood.

He restored a girl to life.

He fed a multitude, thousands in fact, with five loaves and two fish.

Who knew what miracles he would do before their very eyes? Many had questions. But many others believed. The throngs with handicaps and afflictions were there willing to verify the facts and test the doubts. This was a great event—a great show. And, best of all . . . it was free!

There was interest to learn of his gospel. His speech was forthright! He had no fear of authorities or of crowds or of Rome. He spoke his mind. Let the chips settle where they would. Rebuke was often in order. To please or not to please was never the question. Many would be at the heart of his rebuke. The scribes and Pharisees. The landholders and employers. The magistrates and people in authority. If the shoe fit, they were to wear it. History records no apology or a single retraction of any statement. This took nerve. Here was a man with a lot of guts, and it took courage to stand openly before those who were leaders in both Judea and Rome.

Children could crawl between the legs of people. They could step on toes. With little trouble at all they would be in the front line. Those who were big could push their way through a crowd. A shove with a shoulder and arm was sure to bring one to a point of advantage. But if you were very small, and of full age, it would have been impossible for you to see unless a vantage point were available. The tops of buildings, trees, and high points were the best of vantage points. Zacchaeus chose a sycamore tree. Likely, he was not the only one in it. There were others who shared his handicap of size. Here was a servant of Rome, a man of distinction, person of substance, a wielder of wealth and influence, high in a tree.

There were many in that crowd for Jesus to see. The children—he liked them. The handicapped—he was moved with compassion for them. The people—he loved them. And then there were the little people high in a tree. Whom would you have elected?

Jesus turned his eyes to Zacchaeus. He called him by name. He announced that He had chosen to be a guest in Zacchaeus' home. Imagine the attitude of the Romans. Imagine the attitude of the Jews. Imagine the attitude of those with handicaps. Imagine the attitude of the crowd.

Listen to Jesus words: "Zacchaeus, make haste, and come down; for to-day I must abide at thy house" (Luke 19:5).

What would you have done?

Zacchaeus did make haste. He came down. In fact, Luke records the fact that Zacchaeus received him joyfully. And as we could well expect, the crowd murmured. . . . He was going to a man who was a runt. He was going to a man who was a publican. He was going to a man who was a sinner. What would the Nazarene do next?

The Confirmation of Faith

Zacchaeus gave witness to his faith. He believed. So zealous was he in his faith that he climbed a tree to see the one in whom he had so great faith. But even that was not enough. He witnessed to his faith. Listen to his words. "Behold, Lord, the half of my goods I give to the poor; and if I have taken any thing from any man by false accusation, I restore him fourfold" (verse 8).

Quite a witness for one who dealt in assessments. Quite a testimony for one whose professional career was based on taxes. Certainly the career was not known for benevolence or philanthropy. But he stated the fact. He announced his commitment. Not one of tithes or offerings. "Half of what I receive I give to the poor." No strings attached. There is nothing he was to receive in return. Unselfishly, generously, benevolently, and compassionately he shares with the poor. Half of what he has—try that formula for stewardship on for size.

Zacchaeus sometimes wronged people, haven't we all? Sometimes he shortchanged people—received more change than he was entitled to. Sometimes he exacted too great a price. Sometimes he delivered merchandise worth less than the price. What have you done? Trust to luck that others will not know, that you will not be caught, that someone else will make it up, trusting the law of averages that work for us and against us?

But here was Zacchaeus. If someone was wronged, he was repaid four times over. That's a dollar for every quarter. A hundred dollars for every twenty-five. Four thousand dollars for every thousand! Suppose Detroit did that? Suppose Madison Avenue did that? Suppose you did that? What would Jesus say? You are doing too much? Too little? All right?

Here is his great announcement; listen to it carefully— "This day is salvation come to thine house!" Zacchaeus had accepted the Gospel. He had made a commitment. He was keeping the faith.

Salvation was announced after a commitment had been made and faith had been exercised in financial terms!

How does your life compare with that of Zacchaeus? Have you made your commitment? Year after year, in an inflated economy, is your response: "The same as last year?" Are you among those who say, "If I made more I would give?", or "When I get caught up, I'll consider it," or "Wait until the children are grown and married?"

But here was Zacchaeus with a statement of fact: "I give 50 pecent of what I have. When I do wrong, I make recompense four times over.

What were the conditions? There were none. This was the formula. It was at the heart of his faith.

Hear Jesus' response: "This day," as a result of your giving, as a result of your witness, "is salvation come to thine house."

What would you say if Christ were to confront you today? What evidence of faith would he find in your life? What exercise of stewardship would he discern among your resources?

The tragedy lies in the fact that such a meeting is not left to chance. He is here. He confronts you. He invites your witness now!

What can he say of you, your witness, your life?

Zacchaeus stands before us as a model of the Christian faith. His model is what commitment is all about.

You, alone, can provide an answer concerning salvation and your life today.

Beautiful Attitudes

"Blessed. . . . for theirs is the kingdom of heaven."
—The Gospel According to Matthew 5:10

A little girl had been to church and returned to her home only to be confronted by a dinner guest who asked the question, "What did the preacher speak about today?" Her response, "He preached a sermon on the beautiful attitudes." Unable to pronounce the word associated with the great gems from the Sermon on the Mount, she had improvised "beautiful attitudes" for "Beatitudes." It will be her good fortune if each substitute in language and title will be as forthright, descriptive, and appropriate to the situation, for beautiful attitudes are the result of the application of the beatitudes to everyday life; they are intrinsic components in the stewardship of life.

Matthew places the Beatitudes at the very beginning of the Sermon on the Mount and in the homiletical biography of the Nazarene, in the first recorded sermon that the Master was to leave for all posterity. This, together with the prayer pattern for the ages, makes them indelible in the minds and in the hearts of Christians everywhere. They are the spoken word to those in the Judean hills two thousand years ago, and they speak to us now. Listen to what they have to say to us today:

"Blessed are the poor in spirit." It is as though he were saying, "Blessed are the poor—in spirit." Certainly they do not have much, they do not demand much, and they do not expect much. Yet they have happiness.

A pardox in our society lies in the fact that those persons who seemingly have the most to enjoy, appreciate, and be thankful for are the very persons whose lives are beset with restlessness, impatience, and dissatisfaction. Their appetite for the larger, the greater, and the better is never satisfied. Their climb up the ladder of progress is an ascension to a greater level of discontent. Each step of the way, they are demanding more progress and advantage for themselves. The higher they climb, the more remote they are from the kingdom of heaven. Lesser goods eclipse the importance of the significant goal for which there can be no satisfactory substitute.

In my travels across the nation, on many occasions, I have discovered more happiness in Harlem than I have found on Madison Avenue, a greater appreciation for life in Watts than in Burbank, a greater peace of heart and mind in the hills of Appalachia than in the Casinos in Las Vegas.

Blessed are the poor in spirit; they appreciate, enjoy, and understand the opportunities and limitations that society and time provide. This is a product of the stewardship life!

"Blessed are they that mourn." The passing of people, the passing of time, and the passing of landscapes are significant in human progress. A slower step, bowed head, and moistened eye impress us with the fact that we will not pass this way again.

Mourning is indicative of value and appreciation for that which is no longer to be a part of the human experience. Mourning arises out of the sense of loss for those things which will be separated from us by space, time, and circumstances. Often in life we do not appreciate what we have until it is taken from us. Yet mourning is the process of realizing the values of life's priceless gifts in term of relationships, friendships, and associations.

No one can appreciate value and worth unless they perceive what the loss would be in a separation from those things esteemed among us, and it is imperative that Christians be capable of assessing values and recognizing worth in the experiences which make life really worthwhile.

Those who mourn are comforted by the fact that not only is there an appreciation for others, but there is an appreciation for the self by others in the human relationship. This is the very element of life that causes our existence to be Godlike. We become Christlike, then, as we mourn for and with others. We are honored to be Godlike, persons in his image, as others will come to appreciate us. In a society where there is mourning, there is hope for a full appreciation for, and understanding of, human personal relations. This is a product of the stewardship life!

"Blessed are the meek." The poor, as well as those who mourn, find a happy companion in those who are meek. They may not be the drivers, leaders who make the headlines, or persons who serve as the grand marshals of our great parades; but they are in the supporting roles of individuals who are the drivers, leaders who do make the headlines, and persons who are the grand marshals of the great parades. Without their supportive roles there is neither the incentive nor the reason for one to drive. Without the consciousness of their strength, there are no headlines. Without them there is no parade. As such, they are simply those "who inherit the earth."

Societal Watergates remind us that leaders come and go, the mighty are sometimes made to follow, the rich are made lowly. The story has been told so often of the "Tortoise and the Hare," that each is convinced that it is the unassuming that have withstood the heat of the battle, endured the hustle and bustle of the thoroughfares, and, in God's time, attained their appointed place with dignity and honor. No bands playing, no flags flying, no trumpets blowing . . . but the God of eternal values declaring: "Well done, thou good and faithful servant."

It is the meek who inherit the earth, and whether we think of the Stalins, Mussolinis, or Hitlers; the Roosevelts, Churchills, or de Gaulles; it is the unassuming in the Soviet Union, Italy, and Germany, America, Britain, and France who inherit the earth.

Abraham Lincoln once said, "God must have loved the common man because he made so many of them." God loves the meek and their meekness qualifies them to inherit the earth.

Our Lord began his mission with twelve disciples. Another seventy were called also. Two by two, without the benefit of electronics or the printed page, they were instrumental in Christianity's penetrating the frontiers of our first-century societies. None were rulers or diplomats. None were known for their wealth or station. They were, in every sense of the word, common people. The meek . . . they inherited the earth! Meekness was the secret to their success then, and it is the secret to success now and an inseparable quality of the stewardship life.

"Blessed are they which hunger and thirst after righteousness." It does not take a very wise person to cause us to realize that proper nutrition depends upon an appetite for proper things. Jesus, on one occasion, was explicit in saying that his meat and drink was to do the will of God. There is no better feeding for the soul than that which comes through hungering and thirsting after right things.

The appetite for that which is true, honest, just, pure, lovely, and of good report is a product of the Christian life; and the exercise of Christian stewardship is the development of those qualities complementary to our faith and knowledge of our Lord and Savior.

In the course of life, many are tempted to compromise, to be content with the second best. Alternate choices and the lesser good is responsible for much of the imperfection in our society today. Many do not succeed in life, actually do not reach their announced goals in life, simply because they have not held to the mark of the high calling of God in Jesus Christ. Liberal in attitude and yielding in principles, they move from one compromised position to another. Their loss of stature, and questionable integrity, leave them bankrupt among those who sustain a vital witness to the Christian faith. They are less than the person they could and should be.

Those who hunger and thirst after righteousness . . . they shall be filled. Filled with purposefulness, goodness, and the assurance that this life is surely worthwhile. This, too, is inseparable from the stewardship life.

"Blessed are the merciful." The merciful spirit is neither a condescending spirit nor a compromising spirit. The merciful spirit is the spirit that is able to understand the contributing circumstances which lead persons to their human condition and the limitations which have been imposed upon them through the divine-human encounter.

To be merciful does not necessarily mean to approve of a particular condition or situation. Nor does it necessarily mean to condone. To be merciful is to consider the causitive factors, the controlling influences, and the determining agents which surround an individual or group. In this respect we need to remember that there are no exceptions among us to those situations conducive to mercy or the conditions requiring mercy among us. While some factors may govern the human situation for one, other factors will govern the human situation for others. Life is simply that way. As there is a need to be merciful, there is a need to be on the receiving end of mercy. In this respect it seems a component parallel with forgiveness. In the prayer pattern our Lord counseled us to expect forgiveness only to the degree that we are willing to forgive. Mercy is in this court. "Blessed are the merciful for they shall obtain mercy." And this is a product of the stewardship life.

"Blessed are the pure in heart." Purity of heart is a bit different than purity of the body and purity of the mind, for the body and mind are subject always to the exterior forces of life, and we tend to be embellished, controlled, by the five senses. But purity of the heart goes to the very center of the individual, to the very core of our being. The heart is the responsible organ for circulating the blood, and no organ of the body can survive without it. While all are important, Christ and the Gospels place primary value on the heart as the seat of all being. Purity of the heart ensures a potential of purity for the whole of one's being and for the whole of life.

Purity of the heart makes for a consistency with God, and as one evidences purity in heart, there is a quality of being commensurate with the mind and will of God which places the individual in communication with them. So much so, in fact, that the experience is to behold the Divine Presence; and in that very sense of the word, see God! Followers of Jesus were first called Christians in Antioch, for they were understood to be those whose lives were in communication with the Master and those whose purity of heart brought them into a personal relationship with their Lord and Savior. The strangers who visited Abraham were identified as angels; as the pure in heart and they were seen as those whose lives were in communication with the Creator and as a result those of like purpose brought them into a personal relationship with their God and Father. "Blessed are the pure in heart, for they shall see God." This is a product of the stewardship life.

"Blessed are the peacemakers." Conflict is an intrinsic part of human existence. Even in the recitation of beginnings, we are not far into the narrative until we read of envy, jealousy, and hatred. Our first parents, at the Creation, were just a few hours from differences, contests to test the validity of things stated as fact. In a limited period each tested his or her opinion against the opinion of another, even God. Their desires and judgments were not always right, and more often than not, they missed the mark. Instead of ending up in Paradise, misjudgment brought them to a life of difficulty and struggle. Sweat, pain, and tears became the order of the day.

In less than the space of one generation, the documentary reveals division in the human family. Folk separated by rivers, mountains, and seas. And folk separated from each other even in the processes of religious experience. And here a farmer and a rancher are jealous of the assumed pleasure of the Divine Intent, greater for one than for the other. Years of rivalry resulted in a conflict of a moment that ended with pain for one and death for the other.

The biblical narrative is a drama of such struggles and wars. But it is a documentation of those through the years who sought reconciliation. Reconciliation in Egypt, in Babylon, in Israel, and in Judah. Reconciliation between kings and peasants, rich and poor, nations and individuals. And those who were the peacemakers were identified as children of God.

Times have changed, not to an absence from struggle but to a complexity of conflict within the human family. And the total processes of reconciliation become more complex when we consider the difficulty of the human situation, when the instruments for contests are of such great intensity that everyone may be destroyed; the annihilation of all living substances in a matter of minutes.

Peacemakers are required, and are at work, at every level of our societies and our cultures, and their strategies qualify them as the children of God. And this is a product of the stewardship life.

"Blessed are those who are persecuted." Persecuted for being right and for the sake of that which is right. Henry Clay once said that he would rather be right than President. Identification with causes which are right is not always popular. Dedication to principles which must take precedence above all other principles meets with resistance and opposition as ideologies and principles are in conflict. And whether the right prevails or not, it meets with stiff resistance and opposition which makes for abuse and sometimes persecution.

Jesus was certainly no exception. The contest of values, positions, and affirmations went from Bethlehem to Calvary, from local congregations to ecclesiastical councils, from the courts of the temple to the bar of a governor. Often outcast, sometimes isolated, and ultimately crucified, he was pesecuted for righteousness sake; and Easter emphasizes the fact that the ultimate reward is the kingdom of heaven. And this is a product of the stewardship life.

"Blessed are ye when reviled, persecuted, and victimized by malicious and unjust rumors." It is painful when one's integrity is questioned, when one's ideas and ideals are mocked, and when one's reputation is shadowed by malicious gossip. As flood waters flowing from the mountains and over the plains, there is little that one can do about it. The waters must take their course. To dam the tide is merely to seek to arrest or divert the process. When the floodwaters take their course, there is no solution to the problem. Scars and marks will always remain, and many will leave scars and marks of distinction, emblems of credibility and portraits of honor. Many persons, so identified, stand on the horizon of time as giants. Patriarchs, prophets, disciples, and apostles are numbered among their ranks.

The reviled, persecuted, and abused through rumors and gossip gain reward that eternity provides; and time reckons them among the great. This is a product of the stewardship life.

Stewardship is a quality of life inseparable from humility, sobriety, meekness, zeal, compassion, purity, peacefulness, and persistence that history calls beatitudes and a little girl called beautiful attitudes. They are intrinsic components of the stewardship life and are inseparable from our dedication and responsibility as Christians.